Computers A N D Community

Computers

A N D

Community

TEACHING COMPOSITION
IN THE TWENTY-FIRST CENTURY

Edited by

Carolyn Handa

With a Foreword by

Richard A. Lanham

Boynton/Cook Publishers
Heinemann
Portsmouth, NH

BOYNTON/COOK PUBLISHERS
A Division of
HEINEMANN EDUCATIONAL BOOKS, INC.
70 Court Street, Portsmouth, NH 03801
Offices and agents throughout the world

Library of Congress Cataloging-in-Publication Data
Computers and community : teaching composition in the twenty-first century / edited by Carolyn Handa : with a foreword by Richard A. Lanham.
    p.   cm.
    Includes bibliographical references.
    ISBN 0-86709-257-2
    1. English language—Composition and exercises—Study and teaching—Data processing. 2. English language—Rhetoric—Study and teaching—Data processing. 3. Computer-assisted instruction. 4. Word processing in education.
    I. Handa, Carolyn.
PE1404.C6334 1990
808'.042'0285—dc20
                      89-49660
                      CIP

Printed in the United States of America
94 93 92 91 90 9 8 7 6 5 4 3 2 1

For, and in the memory of, our parents

The search for building new possibilities for human relations within both the schools and society will not be an easy one.

—Henry A. Giroux

Contents

 # *Acknowledgments*

I wish to acknowledge the support provided for this project by the Undergraduate Instructional Improvement Program here at the University of California, Davis in the form of travel grants to attend conferences which helped hone my ideas for this book. In particular I wish to thank Dan Wick, Coordinator, Undergraduate Instructional Improvement Programs, and Jay Mechling, Director of the Teaching Resources Center. I also wish to acknowledge the support given by UCD's Committee on Research in the form of a faculty research grant to purchase computer equipment, and by Philip L. Dubois, Associate Vice-Chancellor of Academic Affairs, who continually encourages faculty to find ways to incorporate computers into their instruction.

Eric Schroeder has been an indefatigable colleague and friend. Without his generosity, his encouragement, his faith in my ability to think productively about computers, and his challenging leadership in the computers and composition project here at UC Davis, this book would never have been compiled.

We are all indebted to Peter Stillman, our editor at Boynton/Cook, who believed in this project, helped make it more than just an idea, and saved us from many an egregious error. I myself am grateful to him for his encouragement, his sense of humor, and his willingness to listen.

Most of all, I thank Alexa B. Handa, Stephen Handa, and Paul J. Medlin—who don't really give a cat's whisker about computers, but never fail to comfort and support me far, far above and beyond the call of friendship, no matter what projects I undertake.

C. H.

Foreword

RICHARD A. LANHAM

These exciting and moving reports of a revolutionary composition pedagogy develop a common theme: The most profound
changes wrought by computers in the composition classroom are
social, political, and pedagogical, not technological. Digital technology enfranchises this revolutionary pedagogy but does not mandate it. The technology, all these practicing composition teachers
agree, must be used in a certain way; and they have—working in
very different places and independently—pretty much agreed on
what this way is. Thus their essays, brought together as they are
here, both introduce questions of profound theoretical significance and offer specific guidance about machines and programs,
classroom design, and detailed pedagogical techniques. The authors have come to see, albeit often *per ambages*, that they are
passing through a profound state change in written utterance, but
their feet remain commendably on the ground. No prophetic
mode here; these folks aim to be of immediate use. And, in essays
of consistently high quality, they most certainly succeed. Let me try
first to summarize their collective argument and then to suggest
that perhaps it is even more profoundly revolutionary, more
deeply grounded in the development of Western culture, than they
have chosen to argue here.

As for the computers themselves, keep them simple. The increasingly humble, and increasingly cheap, Mac Plus will do fine,
Schroeder and Boe argue. The machines must be networked so
that every student can talk to every other, and two sorts of programs must enable this: a simple word processor and a conversation program of some sort, again as simple as possible—easy to
learn, easy to use.

As for the classroom, throw out the fixed-seats-facing-a-teach-
er's-podium and substitute clusters of student workstations. Car-

olyn Boiarsky, in an essay sparkling with good sense, suggests that the arrangement common in newsrooms offers the best model.

As for the pedagogy, first of all understand that the instructor's privileged position has been metamorphosed by electronic text. The students write to and for one another, not for the Person Up Front. The success of these classes is measured by how well the students constitute *their own* social and scholarly community. The old Skinner-box conception of computer-assisted instruction (CAI) argued that the teacher would be replaced by an artificially intelligent, tireless electronic robot. The new conception of CAI advanced here offers a more promising replacement—the students themselves. They work collaboratively, as they will do later in the workplace, where too the same boundary conditions of electronic text will apply. The teacher becomes—another new role—a learned coordinator.

The center of this collaborative approach, as Barker and Kemp argue in a strong essay, "is the ability to read student text perspicaciously." Creation and analysis are put into a more balanced oscillation. And electronic text, by filtering out the customary clues of social and sexual hierarchy, allows a more balanced contribution to class discourse by those who usually remain silent. And a further redress of balance is encouraged as well—a balance of authorial motive. Several of the essayists mention that, when the class rather than the instructor becomes the audience, the competitive and performative motives for writing give way to the motive native to digital devices and electronic text—pure play. "Writing doesn't seem so painful when I know that my words are just so many dots of light on a screen," a Middlebury student writes about her writing class. Another says, "I really like 'playing computer' as my roommate has come to call it."

Do the students write better prose when the text is electronic? The authors represented here argue that they do. It is possible to provide a different measure of success, too. Student writers will spend their entire writing lives writing electronic text; that alone is sufficient reason to teach in this way. And still a third measure suggests itself, though these authors only lightly touch on it. The attributes of electronic text to which students are introduced in this new kind of CAI—volatility, interactivity, easy scaling changes, a self-conscious typography, collage techniques of invention and arrangement, a new kind of self-consciousness about the "publication" and the "publicity" that lies at the end of expression (and which several of these teachers exploit through desktop student publishing schemes)—are all the root concepts of postmodernity in twentieth-century arts and letters from the experiments of the Italian Futurists onward to Cage, Warhol, and Robert Graves. To teach writing through electronic text is to put our students deeply in tune with the central tonality of their time. One need not write a song about such a tuning; it just happens. Surely here, too, when we come to think about it, we will find in electronic text the deep link between composition instruction and literary study that we have sought for so long. Indeed, one can foresee a deep linkage with all the arts for, since they have all been digitized, they now group themselves into new patterns of interchangeability, into a new rhetoric of all the arts. It is to such a radically revolutionary design, surely, that the striking pedagogies described in these essays will lead.

Another radical redefinition emerges from these pages which the authors have not yet focused. These students of electronic text are in the process of inventing a new referential form of literacy instruction. For classical antiquity the central form was the oration, an oral form but written as well almost from the earliest days. The Middle Ages, some provocative recent scholarship suggests, adopted the letter as the central genre of instruction. Since Montaigne and Bacon it has been the essay. Now a new form is emerging, as yet called only the humble "file": polyvocal, interactive, volatile—it is indeed still emergent, unfixed. Its exact form is not clear, but clear enough to show that it will not be, as its predecessors have been, an exact form. This new form, which has already penetrated the workplace, may become a scholarly paradigm as well. And students of electronic text are making it part of their second nature.

It is becoming increasingly clear that technology will interact with literacy instruction in our democracy in ways not so deterministic as early thinkers predicted. We will have to *decide* how technology can be orchestrated into socially responsible patterns of use. The essays in this volume illustrate how this essential orchestration can take place, and for this reason they merit the attention of all of us who teach and write about texts.

Introduction

Computers, writing teachers, humanists—an unlikely working trio to the average member of society. Highly unlikely even to the more educated among us. "Humanists are such natural Luddites," Richard Lanham has said, perhaps best describing the dynamic we've come to expect, "and have become so used to regarding technology—and especially the computer—as The Enemy that it takes some temerity to call the personal computer A Possible Friend" (p. 285).

Yet all of us writing in this volume would probably say that the computer is more than a *possible* friend. It actually *is* one—especially because we are teachers. Day after day we struggle through the terrain of muddy compositions hoping somehow to show their writers how to clarify ideas, enliven their prose, and work with their fellow students to do both. We care deeply about how and what we teach our students. Suddenly, as writing teachers and perhaps even more importantly as humanists, we see that the computer offers immense possibility for restructuring relations in both our classes and society. Thus this collection of essays.

The instructors writing here feel that we must approach the computer with some knowledge of its capability for linking working writers, and with some hope for the attitude toward community it can create in a classroom. If we have this knowledge and hope, then we can use the computer as a tool to accomplish our tasks as teachers and as an instrument that conveys our deep concern for the growth and freedom of our students' minds. Some of us feel that we must also bring to the computer some suspicion of the cultural biases and blindnesses inherent in its creation, if only to become less susceptible to them.

It is true that we have written these essays partly for instructors who now teach composition in computer rooms, instructors who use computers to supplement their work in computerless composition classrooms, and instructors seriously considering installing computer labs so they can begin to use computers for teaching composition. But perhaps more importantly, we are also addressing instructors who have never used computers in their classrooms, possibly even never used computers themselves, but who are curious about the pedagogical effects of this particular technology in their classrooms. And ultimately we are addressing all those interested in language studies who may wonder what computers could possibly have to do with community and the ordinary, everyday world we live in.

The seeds for this book were planted some years ago when I began sensing several common fears among a few instructors setting up the first computer classroom for composition instruction at the University of California, Davis. One concern was that as teachers in the humanities we would be incorporating computers in our classrooms at the expense of a social interaction between students that we normally encouraged. But a greater fear was that finally we might turn out students accustomed to an isolated manner of composing, students who would carry with them into society this approach and its attendant attitude toward writing. Given these common fears, a common desire slowly emerged. We wanted to turn our classrooms into places that gradually eroded the stereotype of the socially inept computer nerd/hacker existing deep within the dimly lit labyrinthine cellars of computer buildings. We wanted our students to interact through the computer and to carry over the habit of writing-through-interacting as they continued to write in their careers.

Some of us gradually came to realize that we had slightly political motives too. We wanted our students to see their writing in the context of society and to understand that as writers they always need to be critical (in the literary sense) of that society. I, for one, having been influenced by Richard Ohmann's *English in America*, continued to be bothered by Ohmann's suggestion that I might, in my composition classes, be churning out armies of little bureaucrats who would mindlessly blend into a politically and technologically flawed society. I soon discovered that my colleagues also harbored such fears and desires.

I was specifically moved to solicit this volume's essays after I attended the Conference on College Composition and Communication in March 1987. I wanted to see addressed openly the social concerns that kept emerging as subtexts in various papers delivered at this conference. Many of the speakers seemed to be wondering what *community* is, exactly, and why we felt such an urgent need to remain aware of it as we move into the twenty-first century. Many of us also seemed to be asking ourselves whether or not some of our notions of community may have shifted somewhat in the last half of this century; more and more we appear to be seeing the individual writer less as a solitary composer, secluded and separated from outside influences, than she was previously perceived to be. The image of the secluded writer is a Romantic notion, outworn and suspect at the end of the twentieth century. We live in an age when the individual must learn to balance between valuing self and working with others; today we acknowledge that students learn as much from each other as they do from us.

In fact, we have found that the computer may be a democratic tool. Even in a democracy, society nonetheless provides a multitude of hierarchies, not all of them economic, that cause some people to devalue self, others to privilege self. We take the context of our students' lives much more into consideration now, for we have come to realize how much the communities these students grow up in form their attitudes about writing, including what is "appropriate." To see themselves in context, students must learn to value the self. Otherwise they exclude it from their writing. Some of these students have also been conditioned to protect themselves behind a wall of silence. But we are finding that computer classrooms work effectively to break down some of these misperceptions and barriers. Students who have existed on the margins of discourse are now finding themselves to be central figures.

I realize now that I approached many of this volume's contributors because I sensed the level of their dedication to their students. In addition, because all of the instructors writing here have worked with computers in their composition classes for several years now, they have gone beyond specifically technological concerns; they all realize the connection between technology, pedagogy, and—if only indirectly—politics.

The essays here move from the more practical to the more

theoretical; but the point of view is basically consistent: All the contributors believe the computer is a powerful tool that, if used in certain ways, can not only enhance but create a strong sense of community among both the students and their instructors. If we think of the traditional classroom as having a clearly defined "class" division, that is, a separation between teacher and student built into the physical arrangement of the classroom as well as the pedagogy, then all of the instructors represented here teach in untraditional classrooms. We are trying to control less—to say less that we, as teachers, have the only answers.

The first three essays focus on the architecture of the class-room, the machinery, and the teacher. Thomas Barker and Fred Kemp outline the main points of a new network theory of writing instruction that they feel represents a postmodern pedagogy for our time. They emphasize ways to make composition teaching efficient and enfranchising. In addition, they discuss several "current" teaching strategies to show how these strategies are actually "traditional," indeed ineffective, when we consider the realities of students and funding today. Next, Eric Schroeder and John Boe discuss the various levels of community worth considering when composition programs begin installing computer classrooms—namely, the writing community of students, the community of computer classroom teachers, and finally the entire composition program—and they also address the political implications of populism and minimalism in a computer classroom. Carolyn Boiarsky focuses her chapter on the physical arrangement of the computer classroom and its effect on creating a community of writers. She analyzes several different arrangements to show how fostering a newsroom-style environment can result in changes in pedagogy and students' attitudes.

The next two essays focus more specifically on ways to use the machinery itself to create a sense of community. Carol Klimick Cyganowski explains what an instructor can do with standard word-processing and software packages; she illustrates specific collaborative invention and revision techniques that instructors can use to encourage collaboration. She also comments on changes in attitudes toward the writing process, which she feels

result directly from collaboration and computers. Kathleen Skubikowski and John Elder then focus on how students use a networked Macintosh classroom to explore ways of writing and
discovering their own voices—in particular, how students use computers to foster exploratory writing and exchange and critique
others' writing.

The essays by Mary Flores and by Cynthia Selfe examine conferencing on the computer and begin addressing political issues
that the computer classroom touches on, most specifically a feminist pedagogy. Flores explains how computer conferencing can
help establish feminist goals in a classroom, then bring students to
value their own selves and accept their experiences as valid evidence in their writing. Selfe also touches on computer conferencing but focuses in particular on the breakdown of traditional
patterns of exchange, a breakdown possible especially in a computer classroom. Her paper is important in its call for a theoretical
perspective on the study of computers in composition, one that
would lead us to a liberating vision of computer use in the classroom.

The final two essays discuss issues of empowerment, the
broader implications of computers in a composition classroom,
and the social significance of computer use to teach students
about their language. In describing one of the most powerful
networking projects now operating in the country, ENFI, or "Electronic Networks for Interaction," a multicampus consortium, M.
Diane Langston and Trent Batson explore the many levels of social shifts that begin occurring once we start using computers in a
writing classroom. These begin with teaching modes and strategies
and end with implications for the ways we create, preserve, and
manipulate knowledge. Our conceptions of writers and writing, in
other words, are changing. My own chapter addresses the subject
of the general pedagogical and political considerations instructors
in a computer classroom need to be aware of so that they do not
inadvertently withhold power from their students and condition
them to accept a culture of silence.

Very early versions of some chapters were first presented as
papers at the 4Cs (Conference on College Composition and

Communication—1987), but by now they have been radically altered, if only because of time. Since I first began soliciting these
essays in 1987, much has changed and keeps changing rapidly. All
of the writers here have continued to keep up with technological
developments, to teach, and to refine their ideas accordingly.

WORK CITED

Lanham, Richard A. "The Electronic Word: Literary Study and the Digital Revolution." *New Literary History* 20 (1989): 265–290.

Network Theory: A Postmodern Pedagogy for the Writing Classroom

THOMAS T. BARKER
Texas Tech University
FRED O. KEMP
Texas Tech University

The term *postmodern* can be applied to a variety of cultural phenomena, including artistic style, literary criticism, theology, sociology, and philosophy. The term is complex and we are not so foolish as to attempt a comprehensive definition. Yet for our purposes we find in the uses of the term a common thread of meaning. To us, postmodern suggests a self-conscious acknowledgment of the immediate present and an attempt to respond to it in new ways. More particularly, as Michael Foucault is understood to employ the term, postmodernism suggests a maturing epistemology.

> Knowledge is no longer a result of an individual Cartesian privately examining the certainty of the contents of thought. Instead, it is produced socially, and the individual must be educated into an ongoing discourse, the original questions and motivations of which are either remote and tacit or else themselves the subject of controversy. (Hoy 1988, p. 17)

Richard Rorty, whom Christopher Norris considers one of the most articulate American defenders of the cultural situation that Jean-Francois Lyotard terms "the post-modern condition" (Norris 1985, p. 149), traces his own genesis through Wittgenstein, Dewey, and Heidegger. Each of these "reminds us that investigations of the foundations of knowledge or morality or language or society may be simply apologetics, attempts to eternalize a certain con-

1

temporary language-game, social practice, or self-image" (Rorty 1979, pp. 9–10).

Postmodern in our terms means both a way of looking sensitively and self-consciously at the conditions of the present, and also a means of appropriating new ways of knowing about knowing itself, unencumbered by static assumptions or conventions. A postmodern writing pedagogy represents a structured attempt to combine the realities of current social and economic conditions with instruction that emphasizes the communal aspect of knowledge making.

To begin, we would like to examine some realities surrounding current composition teaching, with particular emphasis on attempts to enfranchise the student in terms of her own education. Various traditional or "current traditional" approaches will be looked at, including methods of providing feedback to students, the debilitating instructional environment we call the "proscenium" classroom, and various failed attempts to enhance student-centered instruction—question and answer, group work, and peer critiquing. We will see that these approaches, although well intentioned, are neither instructionally effective nor responsive to what might be considered the conditions of a postmodern culture, especially regarding reductions in funding and the changing nature of the student population. We then outline the main points of a new *network theory* of writing instruction. Finally, we present a discussion of how network theory uses computers to create a classroom that meets the requirements of a postmodern pedagogy.

CHANGES IN EDUCATION

Our teachers' sense that *something* has changed in American education cannot be gainsaid; things are not as they were in school when they were there, and the students they confront in college classes now are not the same kinds of students *their* teachers confronted in earlier generations. (Foster 1983, p. 81)

David Foster (1983) points out that by the mid-1970s college enrollment had more than doubled since the 1950s. Part of this expansion was a new emphasis on education inspired by the presumed threat of Sputnik, part by the expanded funding of Lyndon Johnson's New Society, and part by a new spirit of egalitarianism in entrance requirements emerging from the societal confusions of the 1960s. Although enrollment figures have fluctuated since, there can be little doubt that this rapid expansion of the college population threw traditional administrative and instructional procedures into disarray. Our classrooms have become ethnically and economically diverse to a degree unimaginable in 1960. Our students in many cases require remediation that the university system has not been designed to provide.

Above all, the open admissions policies resulting from the political and social upheaval of the 1960s has engendered a new ideological awareness among university teachers and students. Guy Benveniste (1985) speculates that because of this new awareness, universities will pay more attention to meeting societal needs. James Berlin argues that even the study of rhetoric demands our ideological awareness, that a "rhetoric can never be innocent, can never be a disinterested arbiter of the ideological claims of others because it is already serving certain ideological claims" (1988, p. 477). Perhaps the most complete view of the effects of open admissions on higher education may be found in Ira Shor's *Critical Teaching and Everyday Life* (1980). Shor examines his own attempts to develop a pedagogy appropriate for the open admissions policy at CUNY. This pedagogy is explicitly based on Shor's struggle to develop an ideologically sound teaching method.

What Shor and others have discovered is that modern students do not bring to their studies the kinds of training and background previously considered necessary. They come from primarily oral strata (Ong 1981) and are often nearly print illiterate. They respond to a democratic model of shared knowledge as opposed to older, elitist models in which knowledge was the privileged possession of certain social groups. To these students, a college education is not only possible, but practically a right guaranteed by society. The instructor is seldom revered as a font of wisdom, but is seen as a functionary dispensing the necessary tools for material success.

Maxine Hairston, in her 1982 CCC article, "The Winds of Change: Thomas Kuhn and the Revolution in the Teaching of Writing," sounded the call for a shift from what she termed the "current-traditional paradigm" of writing instruction toward a paradigm more responsive to research and to the realities of the writing process as it is manifested in unskilled and skilled writers. As an example of the failure of current-traditional methods to address the needs of a rapidly changing student population, she cited the famous struggles of Mina Shaughnessy to cope with CUNY's 1970 shift to open admissions. But Hairston's program, though it generated much enthusiasm and stimulated a considerable corrective action against the more blatant current-traditional practices then existing, nevertheless fell short of a pedagogy that seriously addresses the epistemological issues of a postmodern view of knowledge, her use of Kuhn notwithstanding.

Another reality to be faced is decreased funding in many of our colleges and universities. James Mingle (1981) notes that many universities will experience declines in revenue, or at least in traditional revenue sources. The financial environment is shrinking partly because other state institutions are claiming state funds (Benveniste). A problem with encouraging greater funding lies in the fact that universities are labor intensive. Productivity gains are slow to come and hard to see. The result is that the higher costs of education are unmatched by an increase in funds. Whether or not we agree with Benveniste that universities will be more politically active in the future, we still should recognize, in order to compete with other state agencies for funding, the changes these realities portend. A computer-based postmodern pedagogy clearly indicates to legislators the aggressive desire for progress on the part of instructors and administrators and their willingness to employ modern technology and the lessons of our new information and service economy.

WHAT WE SHOULD DO

It is not our intention to chart an improved course for higher education. The trends noted here are influenced by much more than composition pedagogy. And yet we do need a pedagogy for our time. R. C. Townsend, as far back as 1970, noted the "need to reconsider the traditional cultural assumptions informing the English curriculum" (p. 718). Recent changes in enrollment and funding give greater urgency to our concerns for a new, postmodern pedagogy: a pedagogy adapted to the demands of our time. From what we have seen, what might be the unmistakable hallmarks of such a pedagogy?

On the one hand, a postmodern pedagogy of writing should be enfranchising in nature. The current student population appears to view college as a means to an end, as a transition place from one social level to another. These students require a teaching method oriented toward advancement in business and industry. Additionally, because many students come from areas outside the traditional student sector—areas that are, in many cases, politically unenfranchised and economically deprived—our pedagogy should be open, inclusive, nonhierarchical, consensus based, and process oriented. Such instruction would bring students into the intellectual enterprise in a real way, without transforming them into what we may misconceive to be intellectuals.

On the other hand, a new pedagogy of writing should be efficient. It should use faculty labor more productively than in the past, and it should use technology, in the form of computers, for instance, to make teaching more effective. In this way it can help make colleges and universities more competitive for government funding. A new pedagogy should respond to the high costs of classroom instruction. In addition, as Mingle points out, planning in the area of higher education should consider a *system perspective* that will allow for the goals of writing instruction to join with the contributions and goals of other university programs. Finally, a pedagogy for the modern student should establish the university or higher education system as part of the service economy that has developed from the information explosion of the past 20 years. We should show ourselves responsive to the student as consumer (Riesman 1980).

On a more limited level, we also need to respond to theoretical advances that reflect the realities of the postmodern composition classroom. Apart from the process-oriented teaching that has grown in popularity during the past 10 years, we should be cognizant of the social-constructionist thinking of writers like Kenneth Bruffee and James Berlin. Their work has important implications for any postmodern pedagogy, in that it provides us with a widely supported theoretical framework. In particular, it allows us to articulate an epistemology—a way of knowing—that includes student and teacher in a knowledge-making enterprise. Such a way of discussing classroom interaction has, as we shall see, important implications for how we design the classroom of the future.

THE TRADITIONAL WRITING CLASSROOM

The traditional writing classroom presumes that the students are the writers and the instructor (or grader) is the sole reader. The only channel for formal written communication, therefore, moves from students to instructor. The students gain insight into how effective their writing is through the *fourfold feedback*: grades, editing symbols, margin comments, and writing conferences with the instructor. Students are expected to write frequently with little sense of what it means to be on the receiving end of all their writing. Their need to revise or their feeling for revision itself depends wholly on their interpretation of the *fourfold feedback*. The student, therefore, never learns to revise in accordance with his or her own interpretation of the text, but always in accordance with his or her interpretation of the instructor's interpretation of the text.

Such a process emphasizes the instructor and the instructor's reading of the text at the expense of the student and the student's reading of the text. This current-traditional approach presumes that the student learns best to write perspicaciously by following the precepts of the instructor, delivered no matter how idiosyncratically through the *fourfold feedback*. What this approach engenders, however, is not emulation of the instructor, but rather a sense of distance from one's own text. In the current-traditional classroom, writing is not so much to be read as to be evaluated; the effectiveness of any text lies not in the power of persuasion and description, but in its ability to trigger highly conventionalized responses from professional graders. James Britton and his colleagues refer to this type of writing as "writing for an examiner audience" (p. 197). In normal circumstances, the teacher

> is not, however, simply a one-man audience but also the sole arbiter, appraiser, grader and judge of the performance. He becomes an audience on whom pupils must focus a special kind of scrutiny in order to detect what they must do to satisfy him. . . . Indeed the writer is frequently placed in the position of telling the reader what the latter already knows more fully and more deeply. (Britton, p. 64)

This process, in effect, "neutralizes" the power inherent in written expression. Current-traditional instructors complain that students "have nothing to say," and yet they themselves have carefully taught students to say the same thing over and over again: "Who cares what I am writing about; just give me a good grade." Unless the current-traditional teacher happens to be highly committed and have an exceptionally strong personality, current-traditional instruction inevitably produces stultifyingly conventional behavior on the part of both students and instructors.

In addition, such an approach does not accommodate the modern student. Instead, it harkens back to an older era in which college students were fewer and consequently better prepared by secondary school classwork. As members of a recognized elite, they were highly motivated to learn and benefited from the "top-down" and "information transfusion" instructional models.

The "top-down" or deductive approach provides students descriptions of generalized or abstracted behavior and expects students then to particularize the abstractions into specific writing behaviors. This approach is characterized by classroom lectures and extensive reading assignments from writing texts. Although favored by most academics, the top-down approach has been shown to be highly ineffectual with many (if not most) student groups. In educational parlance, most students "accept" whatever information is dished out to them (as evaluated by objective tests), but often fail to "internalize" it, or transfer the information into productive behaviors. The top-down approach is the usual one in academic instruction and supposes a kind of student with an intellectual, top-down grasp of knowledge and problem solving. This kind of student is, even in academia, in the minority. The egalitarian emphasis in higher education in the United States makes the "top-down" or "information transfusion" approach to instruction inappropriate for many of our classes.

As we continue to examine the current-traditional approach to composition teaching, we find not only an inappropriate approach to learning, but an inappropriately structured environment. The traditional classroom assumes a rectangular or occasionally wedge shape in which student desks are positioned to focus the attention of the students forward and to the center. The model for such an arrangement is theatrical. In some large classes, proscenium lights are turned on and the instructor becomes privileged not only by position but also by lighting. In large classes, too, the instructor may use a microphone, either fixed or portable, to make herself heard. Most often the blackboards are positioned immediately behind the instructor, and so are various audiovisual screens.

In public schools, this forward "stage" or focus of classroom attention is usually the location of an American flag, flags, or mottos of the school, and lists of classroom rules. So, too, in college classrooms, signs that indicate "no smoking" and the like are fixed high on the forward wall. In some college classrooms of our experience, the "stage" literally consists of a platform six to eight inches high on which the instructor's desk is situated, so that even when seated the instructor's head rises above those of his students. In other, usually large classrooms, just as in most theaters, the floor is sloped toward the proscenium to allow the students a clear field of vision. In many college classrooms, there is some kind of lectern, usually portable, on which the instructor places notes or text and lectures while standing.

Such arrangements produce the environmental equivalent to having students write only to instructors. That is, classrooms such as those just described overwhelmingly reinforce the notion that the instructor is the master of the room, the arbiter of classroom action, and the source of whatever value the room (and the instructional experience) holds. From the first minute of class, the students literally look to the instructor for explicit and implicit clues to how they will be expected to behave in order to succeed, using what Britton called above "a special kind of scrutiny." The body language of the instructor—her frowns, her impatient sighs, her benevolent gaze out over the students, the force with which she writes her name on the board, the *way* in which she writes her name on the board, the title she gives herself, the size of the lettering, the lettering itself—all constitute means by which, unconsciously or consciously, the instructor begins to mold student behavior. Is the instructor tough? easy? precise? Is she gentle? Will she demand much of her students or will she generally "leave them alone" (much as many of them would love simply to leave her alone)?

The students, quite unconsciously, have learned in their years of schooling to read teachers much more proficiently than to read textbooks, and they have learned that success or failure depends much more on that reading than on what is assigned. The traditional classroom suggests nothing else. Just as in a theater we expect to be manipulated by the actors and the script, students in traditional classrooms expect to be manipulated by instructors and their curricula. Just as good actors engage us in their dilemmas, ambitions, and justifications, good teachers engage students in the ambitions and justifications of the teachers themselves. And if these ambitions and justifications serve the community and the individuals in that community well, then good teachers serve their students well.

The problem is that, just as there are only a few really good actors, there are only a few really good teachers. Then, too, the purpose of education at whatever level is not to indoctrinate students in the lofty goals and methods of exemplary people, but to challenge students to develop their own goals and methods and to provide them means to do so. We as postmodern educators should not be trying to "make" lawyers and teachers and businessmen so much as trying to provide students the processes and practices that will allow them to make themselves into whatever they wish to be.

This "self-creation" is not a function of transmitted information and knowledge. It is, rather, a function of how relevant knowledge within real-world contexts is developed. That is, we should not be trying to fill students with transfused facts and abstract principles, but instead give students (1) practice in recognizing situations in which new knowledge is required and (2) practice in producing such knowledge by negotiating information within contexts. We need to teach students not "what" they need to know, but "how" they will produce what they need to know when relevant occasions arise.

The proscenium classroom cannot escape from emphasizing the "what" of information over the "how" of forming knowledge. It is geared to the lecture model and to information transfusion. The instructor in such a classroom is the undoubted source of knowledge, of proper behavior, and of values (as the acknowledged evaluator). Attempts have been made in the past to mitigate this so-called teacher-centered instruction and substitute instead a "student-centered" instruction, but none very effectively.

For instance, for some years educators have emphasized a "question–answer" mode over a "lecture" mode. Most serious commentators agree that lectures generally fail to engage the general student and therefore make learning a deadly passive affair. Except for highly motivated students who bring a relatively sophisticated knowledge of the subject (and hence an already defined context) into the lecture hall, the student victims of lectures either tune out the drone or immerse themselves in prodigious note taking. Notes are a way of supplementing long-term memory in the struggle to preserve the information transfusion, but as countless pedagogues have observed, notes are next to useless when they represent transcribed facts as opposed to immediate personal responses. The difficulty with note taking as a useful exercise is that the student must first have personal responses, and such responses require a relatively sophisticated prior knowledge and an already defined context.

Question–answer as an instructional technique is supposed to relieve the inherently passive nature of lectures by requiring listeners to provide an occasional personal response. The lecturer controls the nature of the responses by asking more-or-less specific questions. In a sense not usually defended, however, question–answer does constitute progress over the straight lecture mode, especially if the instructor calls on students randomly. The students now recognize a new enervating tension in the room. At any point a student may be required to demonstrate publicly that he or she has actually been listening. This danger to some degree precludes a conscious "tuning out" of the lecture on the part of the students in order to avoid the ridicule of being caught daydreaming (although modern students seem much less troubled making the admission "I wasn't listening" than students of previous times). This kind of question–answer performs much the way tests do—as a method of enforcing effort. Ideally, of course, questions should be asked and answers given as a means of responding to the confusions of the students and directing the course of the presentation, and occasionally question–answer performs this way. Usually, however, question–answer reinforces the notion of teacher as "examiner."

In any case, the instructor remains the pivotal agent in question–answer. She produces the questions and she evaluates the answers; she directs the class dynamic, and no student would doubt that. Question–answer does provide an opportunity, however, for students to attempt their one technique of asserting power (aside from outright disruption), and that is the universally revered attempt to get the teacher "off the subject." If the students can shake the instructor free of his subject matter long enough to engage him on some pet topic or personal experience, then they, not he, have assumed control over the class dynamic, and it has been the experience of many that when such diversion occurs, the interest and energy of the students rise quickly. It may be that the students recognize implicitly that they are at last asserting some control and respond with understandable pleasure, or it may be that the instructor is more animated in presenting personal as opposed to scholarly material. Many instructors have even been known to stimulate presentations by faking digressions, allowing students to sidetrack them into remarks that students believed were irrelevant but were actually pertinent to the thesis of the presentation. Such reverse psychology is hardly an adequate instructional technique, however, since students soon catch on and, as always, resist manipulation.

A technique more effective than question–answer in decentralizing the classroom has manifested itself generally as group work. Writers representing the best of those promoting group work, such as Sharan, Gere, and Johnson, report considerable success using this method. In group work the class is broken up into groups of three, four, or five students. The groups are then given assignments to be completed collectively. Each group may assume responsibility for the organization and incrementalization of tasks relevant to its assignment, including invention, source-work, and preparation of the final document. For instance, a major application of group work occurs in the area of invention, outlined by Karen LeFevre (1987) as one of four perspectives on invention. In her taxonomy of perspectives, LeFevre identifies "collaborative" invention as a situation in which writers interact to invent and to create a resonating environment for writing.

The problems with implementing group work in the traditional environment can be summarized as follows:

1. The proscenium classroom provides a poor environment for group work. If desks are fixed to the floor, then collaborating students must twist in their seats or sit on desk surfaces simply to face each other as a group. If desks can be positioned into circles, then four or five groups must hold discussions in the same room at the same time. Noise and distraction abound, and no one can escape the suggestion that this is traditional instruction in a traditional classroom within the traditional class period but disguised as project work (which usually is driven not by the *form* of the encounter, but by the nature of the required tasks).

2. If the instructor attempts to avoid the domination of classroom form by requiring groups to meet outside of class time at their own instigation in a place of their own choosing, then some students, especially nontraditional students, may be forced by circumstance to miss such meetings, and these and others may resent the imposition of required attendance outside of scheduled class meetings.

3. Often, one or two members of a group assume an inordinate responsibility for the group effort, in effect dominating the efforts of others. Equally often, one or two members of a group simply refuse to contribute their share. Many times, the personalities of group members intrude to subvert the instructional objectives envisioned by the instructor. The resulting inequities of contribution or personality

conflict often require the instructor to intervene and generate individual motivation outside the dynamic of the group, in effect subverting most if not all of the purpose for group work itself.

4. If the group is to produce together, then it should be evaluated as a whole, but because of the reasons cited above and a general feeling that students should be graded on individual merit, any attempt to grade group work is slated for deep difficulty. If individuals are to be graded for their individual effort, then the members of a group quickly realize that the group as an instructional entity is a fiction; they may proceed through collaborative motions, but in the end they will be evaluated as always, as individuals turning in individual work. The instructor who would require group work but grades on an individual basis is faced with a very difficult administrative situation. If, on the other hand, all the individuals in a group are to receive the same grade (the grade that the group itself receives), then the instructor must be prepared for a wide range of moral, ethical, and even legal challenges.

Another attempt to produce a student-centered instruction is one that involves what once was called "peer editing" but that, with the growing depreciation of grammar and editing skills, has become "peer critiquing." The operating concept behind peer critiquing is that students should write papers not for the instructor but for each other, and that criticism should therefore come from other students, not the instructor. The concept envisions two advantages to peer critiquing: (1) Writers have readers whose opinions, because of the usual dynamics of peer interaction, they take seriously in terms of what is actually read and understood, as opposed to what is professionally evaluated—what we call "de-neutralizing the text"; and (2) critiquing papers written by one's peers more readily leads to close and considerate reading of one's own text than does reading model essays or ingesting abstract "advice."

A further argument for instruction that employs peer critiquing is that such instruction more closely models the demands of the "real world" than does the highly artificial nature of instructor grading. Professional writing, by almost all accounts, is the product of the writer's conscious association with members of a particular professional group. This is shown specifically by the acknowledgments given at the beginning of a book and by the numerous citations and references provided throughout, and more generally by any special terminology used. Writers write as participants of a particular group of people who share the same general assumptions and vocabulary—what is sometimes called a "discourse community." Managers, in order to write to others in their company, must successfully read and employ assumptions about communication and management likely to be understood by other managers, or executives. Books that are meant for the "lay" population must be translated from a discourse-specific terminology into the terms and concepts comprehensible to the widest possible community.

Students who generate their own theses in order to contribute to the idea pool of a discourse community and who clarify and modify those theses in response to the genuine reactions of that community eventually establish themselves as a significant element in the knowledge making of the community. They assume partial responsibility for how that community views the world and its particular activities within that world. They accept the challenges such responsibility brings, and see their verbal presentations, oral or written, as the principal device for meeting such challenges. Words are power, but students who are forced to use words in meaningless exercises never realize that. The effect of their words on anyone besides the instructor, who functions as simply a professional extension of the exercise, goes unrealized.

Group work and peer critiquing are often mixed in various ways and to various degrees, but much the same problems plague each attempt to decentralize the classroom. For one thing, students critique each other's papers with varying degrees of effort and skill. Lacking the reading or editorial skills of teachers (or the specific occupational motivation of teachers), many students are simply at a loss when it comes to reading critically. They ape editorial remarks as well as they can, and generally fall back on vague affirmations or rejections ("I like your ideas." "You have problems expressing yourself."). When prompted to respond to the position or thesis the student writer advocates, many peer editors can't discern a position or thesis, even when one is clearly evident to the instructor.

Peer critiquing, like group work (with which it is often combined) and, to some degree, the question–answer method, attempts to shift the responsibility from the instructor to the student for the generation, exchange, and evaluation of ideas and expression in the class. Although the psychological theories that support attempts to decentralize the classroom and deneutralize the text seem intuitively right, the sheer *managerial* problems of reducing the dominance of the instructor by empowering the student seem insurmountable. And in the traditional proscenium classroom, they are.

The instructional methodologies described above represent the best of our pedagogical thinking so far, but, given the realities of the modern student and the environment of financial retrenchment surrounding our universities, they fall short of the goals of enfranchising and efficiency. And, we agree, part of the blame for the deficiency may be laid to the exigencies of the traditional classroom: its box-like nature and its unmanageability. However, the previous discussion helps us identify the path to a new, postmodern approach that, we think, responds to the new model of writing instruction.

NETWORK THEORY

Before we describe the classroom application of the new model in detail, let us state as clearly as we can what we believe to be the basic tenets of what we call *network theory*.

The essential activity in writing instruction is the textual transactions between students. These transactions should be so managed by the network as to encourage a sense of *group knowledge*, a sense that every *transactor* influences and is influenced by such group knowledge, and a sense that such group knowledge is properly *malleable* (responsive to the influences of each transactor). The result of textual transactions so managed is a *deneutralizing* of text itself and a greater emphasis and skill on the part of the transactor in rendering such text.

The usual complaint against using computers pedagogically in the classroom is that they isolate students, removing them from the effective instructional activity of the group to stare at video screens and to perform automated drill and practice. Actually, the exact opposite occurs when computers are networked and programmed to manage text transactions between class members.

In the proscenium classroom, the students face the instructor. All verbal transactions proceed through the instructor, so one might diagram the dynamic of a proscenium classroom by drawing straight lines from each student to the instructor. Even when the class is engaged in a "discussion" (as every teacher knows), the management of remarks—and most of the clarification and direction—belongs to the instructor. The only time one might actually diagram student verbal transactions by drawing lines directly between students without proceeding through the central switchboard is when discussions are appropriated by the students themselves, the topic "gets out of control," and the instructor becomes superfluous. Seldom does this happen in a felicitous way, and usually the instructor, after tolerating a careening discussion for a few minutes, reasserts control and brings students back to the "point." It is most difficult for students to see themselves as anything but manipulated, and hardly the self-directed "knowledge makers" of real-world discourse.

The computer-based classroom, when networked using an egalitarian instructional system such as the Daedalus Instructional System, provides a different diagram. Here, the links or lines of contact proceed from every workstation to every other workstation. No link is privileged. There is no master control over them. If the instructor wishes to participate in the discourse, she must choose a workstation and participate at a transactional level equal to that of any other person sitting at any other workstation. The instructor can sit at the "front" of a classroom (if such can be defined), at the "back," or anywhere. Networked microcomputers dissolve the proscenium classroom. The shape of the room and the placement of the workstations are of no (or very little) consequence.

Realistically, of course, the instructor retains a considerable authority by virtue of her ultimate responsibility for curriculum and evaluation and classroom discipline, but her removal from the *position* of authority at the front and from the role of transactional switchboard greatly emphasizes the role of individual students as knowledge makers and empowered participants in the discourse of the community (as defined by the network). Theoretically, the same effect could be obtained by simply sticking 20 students into a proscenium classroom in which the desks have been scrambled and in which the instructor remains seated at one of the desks without uttering supervisory remarks. But without the *management* provided by the collaborative software, whatever interaction takes place would probably collapse into the kind of undirected social discourse one finds at a party.

The instructional system software, therefore, manages the verbal transactions of the networked computer-based classroom in a way that is roughly analogous to the instructor who stands at the front of a proscenium classroom and directs activities, but with many advantages over such a traditional situation. In contrast to stereotypical expectations, networked instructional systems generate many times more student-to-student transactions than traditional instruction, even when such traditional instruction is augmented by peer critiquing and group work. These transactions generally take three forms, as *formal text*, as *electronic mail*, and as *electronic discussion*.

Formal text: Written on a word processor, these are documents that correspond to the theme, essay, journal entry, or position paper of traditional instruction. These documents are written in response to an assignment given either by the instructor or by a group. When the document is judged ready to be "published," it is uploaded to a database of documents accessible by the entire network. Although we believe that simply writing on a word processor greatly enhances one's writing power by emphasizing revision and writing as process, the present description is concerned with computers only as text-communicating or text-sharing devices.

"Publication" of student text in noncomputer collaborative instruction requires prodigious copying and hand-to-hand distribution of text, and for this reason most such publication is limited to a few copies for one peer critiquing group. In the networked computer-based classroom, however, simply by uploading text to the document database, the student has made her document instantly and quite easily accessible to the entire class, or even to other classes who use the network. Five hundred can read the document as easily as five. If the instructor has directed the management software to do so, any of those with access to a particular document—as few or as many as the instructor decides—can download the document onto their own diskettes for on-line annotation or for perusing on compatible computers not on the network. Documents can also be printed out by the reader to be read and commented on without the use of a computer at all.

Whenever a shared document database is described to those not very familiar with computer use, the fear often arises that documents may be altered maliciously or that documents can be too easily plagiarized. In fact, documents stored in a database can easily be "locked" and changes prevented by anyone except the author, even though the document can be read by anyone. And, since documents are so readily accessible, plagiarism is largely eliminated. With so many readers reading each document, plagiarists have many more chances of being discovered than if documents were being read only by instructors.

Even if the network performed no other function than to share formal text, such text would be powerfully "deneutralized" since the writer would be well aware of the public nature of his work from the first word written. As the writer reads the shared text of his classmates, he becomes increasingly aware of how his own ideas and his own presentation fit into the context of his particular discourse community. He accomplishes this without being subject to information transfusions containing top-down generalizations or abstract principles. We believe that irrespective of further pedagogical measures, the sharing of text easily promotes the power of text, which in turn motivates and directs the writer in instructionally effective ways.

Electronic mail: The uploading of formal text, such as essays and reports, into a document database roughly corresponds to its publication for general readership. The sending of electronic mail, however, corresponds to communicating by office memo or by personal, less carefully crafted comments. Formal text is usually drafted on a word processor and revised and edited many times before being uploaded into the document database. It may include a complex and subtle analysis of some wide-ranging issue. Mail, on the other hand, is written quickly and sent to a specific addressee, who can be anyone in the class or, if the instructor is widening the community to other sections, anyone at all with access to the network. Mail is usually limited in content to one topic or controlling idea.

The content of a mail message is limited only by restrictions imposed by the instructor, but mail is generally used as a "peripheral" channel of communication between a reader and a writer involving reactions to a piece of formal text. If an essay is to be read and critiqued, then electronic mail is the means by which the critiques are transmitted and responded to. The way this usually works in practice is that a student enters the mail program and asks to see a particular document stored in the document database. This document appears in the upper half of the computer screen and can be scrolled up and down, beginning to end. The student then asks to send a mail message to the author of the document. An editing box, or scratch pad, appears in the lower half of the screen. The student reads the document in the upper half of the screen while entering comments in the bottom half. When she has finished commenting, she sends the bottom half off to the network as a mail message. When the writer of the formal text enters the mail program, he sees that he has mail, calls up the message, and, if he wishes, responds to the message using the same split-screen technique that was used to critique his essay.

Ideally, a reader's mail to a writer commenting on some aspect of the writer's document will stimulate a correspondence or give and take between the reader and writer that will influence the ideas and presentation of the writer and lead to a revision of the original document. Or, a number of readers may send mail to a writer commenting on his document in such a way that he is able to synthesize a general reaction that will influence a revision. If a writer is able to justify or clarify elements of an essay in subsequent responses, then he should see the need to include those justifications or clarifications in the original document.

Using electronic mail for communicating critiques is not conceptually different from the sort of margin commenting or face-to-face interaction that takes place in noncomputer peer critique sessions. But there are three major differences between networked computer-based critiquing and traditional peer critiquing that emphasize the advantages of using computers.

1. The comments are all delivered in text, usually complete sentences. On the one hand, this proves an advantage over margin comments for it makes understanding the comments much easier, since the writer doesn't have to translate brief and often cryptic phrases. On the other hand, having the remarks in text provides a considerable advantage over oral exchanges, for not only are the remarks generated at the critic's own pace, with the ability to revise and clarify, but also the author of the essay ends up with a permanent copy of those remarks to reread and study. Specific points of disagreement can be pinned down and closely examined. The loss of the spoken word may seem to inhibit the immediacy of the criticism and reaction, but the convenience of transmitting e-mail (which can be sent and read independently of class meetings) replaces one kind of immediacy with another. In addition, the direction of the commenting is not all one way, since the author can respond with his own mail message. The possibility of a considered exchange taking place over days and even weeks provides a whole new opportunity for sustained inquiry concerning a document or issue.

2. The fact that all exchanges are recorded in text means that even in discussing and reacting to formal text, students are practicing writing. The confinement of all (or most) verbal activity to written text is what we call *textualizing* the class. The advantages to textualizing are myriad, but in general include the following: The student necessarily gains more fluidity in expressing herself in written text than if most of her critiquing were done orally; text itself is not restricted only to formal (and, to some students' minds, artificial) expression, but becomes equated with real points and real ideas responding to specific challenges; and the fact that all remarks are by definition transcribed enforces a seriousness and self-consciousness on the part of the commentator.

3. Using the computer as a communication medium "purifies" informal exchanges in interesting and pedagogically advan-

tageous ways. We call this *psychological filtering*. Filtering arises when a person uses a computer to communicate with another person, either through electronic mail or through electronic discussion. Many aspects of face-to-face communication are filtered out when the computer becomes the medium of exchange. These include body language, intimidating or distracting appearances, voice and intonation, aggressive or distracting speech mannerisms, quick- or slow-wittedness, and all the paraphernalia that allows physical context to intrude on and inhibit the pure exchange of ideas.

We have found that the dominating person has a much more difficult time dominating text exchanges than oral exchanges, and conversely, the shy person much more easily advances comments through a computer than in person. The dynamics of personal interaction lose their peaks in a computer-mediated environment, providing a situation that encourages a classroom verbal activity more akin to formal written expression and less akin to informal discussion. Undoubtedly, the strong personality suffers in the psychologically filtered instructional environment, and the one who suffers most may be the instructor. Nevertheless, the requirement that interactive dynamics be indicated textually instead of orally provides one more serious emphasis on writing.

Electronic discussion: Mail messages exist in *file time*, which means that when a message is sent it is stored in a special mail database waiting to be summoned by the addressee. It can sit there for five minutes or five months before the addressee calls up the message and reads it. Similarly, any response of the addressee is stored in the mail database awaiting a specific instruction to be read. But messages can also be sent immediately, or in *real time*. In this case, when Student A sends a message, that message appears simultaneously on every monitor in the computer-based classroom. When Student B reads the message on his monitor, she calls up an electronic scratch pad (editing box), writes a response, and sends it. The message of Student B then appears on every monitor in the room directly below that of Student A. A message sent by Student C at another computer would appear directly below that of Student B on every monitor in the classroom, and so forth, with all subsequent messages sent by anybody in the class. Except when a student is composing a message to send, all the monitors in the class reflect the same scrolling message stream—a stream to which anyone in the class can add at will.

The discerning reader will see that such a discussion could be quite chaotic, with students constantly adding comments to a scrolling stream of messages, and, indeed, early electronic or real-time discussion programs were quite chaotic. But more recent electronic discussion programs, such as Daedalus Interchange, provide a number of features that control and clarify the classroom dynamic and make electronic discussion perhaps the most exciting and effective computer-based pedagogical device used.

For one, any student at a computer can stop the messages scrolling or can scroll back to read previous messages, actions that allow her to review selected messages and pick up on any interesting discussion threads. Any student can also establish a "subconference" and publish its existence, so that those interested in a particular aspect of the discussion can restrict the stream of messages appearing on their screens to just their group. These students can, of course, rejoin the "main conference" whenever they like. Following an electronic discussion session, all comments made are placed in one file and a transcript printed, if desired.

There are a number of advantages to electronic discussion over traditional classroom discussions, including the *textualizing* and *psychological filtering* mentioned above. Perhaps just as important as either of these is the multiplexity of student interaction possible with electronic discussion. Whereas traditional classroom discussions are restricted to a serial interaction, or one speaker after another, electronic discussion allows (even encourages) a parallel interaction, or many "speakers" commenting at the same time. The computers arrange the input into a rapidly expanding stream of comments and then provide "windows" into the stream and the means by which the comments can be negotiated by each participating individual. That is, the reader in electronic discussion is no longer at the mercy of the speaker or whoever sets the agenda of speakers (usually the instructor), but can peruse discussion points at will, selecting times and places in which to intervene and challenge what has been presented.

Programs such as Daedalus Interchange can also call up other documents on a split screen, export interesting comments from the message stream into other files, and even call up the mail program so that file-time messages can be personally addressed and sent even in the midst of a real-time discussion. The transcripts of electronic discussion sessions, which can run as long as 30 or 40 pages of single-spaced text, can and have been used to stimulate further electronic discussion sessions, as transcribed brainstorming for invention purposes, or even as ingenious source material for final exams.

Undoubtedly electronic discussion is a difficult process to envision, and perhaps even more difficult to defend in a description such as this, but electronic discussion has been used for years at schools such as the University of Texas at Austin, Gallaudet, Carnegie-Mellon, New York Institute of Technology, Northern Virginia Community College, and most recently at Texas Tech University, Lynchburg College, and the University of Indiana–Purdue University at Indianapolis. As these schools have reported, the instructional possibilities of this type of student interaction are limited only by the imagination of the instructors who employ them.

The network theory described above, we think, meets the demands of today's students in being enfranchising, open, and egalitarian in its emphasis. And we have seen that the management of classroom activities provided by the computer-based instructional software can help us meet the requirement of an efficient, systematic methodology. In the remaining section of this chapter we outline a pedagogical approach called *the computer-based collaborative approach*. Built on network theory and supported by a networked computer classroom, this approach represents an application of postmodern pedagogy to classroom needs.

THE COMPUTER-BASED COLLABORATIVE APPROACH

The underlying tenet of the computer-based collaborative approach is that the most important skill in good writing is the ability to read student text perspicaciously. The student must, in other words, be a good reader of student text in order to be a good writer of student text, and such a skill depends on plenty of both unstructured and structured practice reading student papers.

Good writing, therefore, is a function of revision, but revision itself is a function of (1) purpose and motivation, (2) awareness of voice and audience, and (3) the conscious application of editing skills. The computer-based collaborative approach supposes that the one instructional activity that best supports these elements of revision is the intense reading and critiquing of peer texts.

There are three theoretical steps (or "levels") the student passes through toward completion of the course. These are

1. Attitude shift
2. Assimilation of revising behaviors
3. Application of discourse conventions

The *attitude shift* occurs when the student comes to recognize the power of the text, when the reading of peer texts enforces a "deneutralizing" of writing. The *assimilation of revising behaviors* occurs when the student comes to recognize the effectiveness of revising protocols, and this is largely a function of revision exercises (word-processing exercises) and critique heuristics. The *application of discourse conventions* occurs when the student comes to recognize that the effectiveness of any text depends on a proficient compliance with the editorial traits of a particular type of prose. This recognition is largely a function of textbook instruction and instructor critiquing.

The computer-based collaborative approach attempts to reempower text by emphasizing the student text itself instead of the instructor's evaluation. Computers are used to facilitate the generation and distribution of both original writing and written student responses to that writing. As students grow aware of how they themselves respond to the words and phrases of their peers, they grow more aware of how their own words are being read.

Accordingly, writing and revision become not simply a mandated exercise, but an opportunity to shape the opinions of one's readers, readers with whom the writer identifies. Writers are encouraged to write as experts to a various and unknown audience. Often in our classes writers write to students in other classes and maintain "written conversations" discussing course topics with them through e-mail. Occasionally we have used wide-area networks like Bitnet and Internet to provide text sharing between campuses. The computer-based collaborative approach taps into a natural human desire to say real things to "real people," a designation we more readily allow our peers than those with whom we have little sympathy.

The computer-based collaborative approach eschews the top-down, "information transfusion" concept of writing instruction, or what Seymour Papert, the MIT mathematician and inventor of the instructional programming language Logo, has called "teaching by advice." It has been our experience that writing instruction must be "bottom-up" and not "top-down." Papert, in *Mindstorms* (1980), describes the failure of an instructional system dependent on the proscenium classroom and the teacher as examiner: "The intellectual environments offered to children by today's cultures are poor in opportunities to bring their thinking about thinking into the open, to learn to talk about it and to test their ideas by externalizing them" (p. 28). The computer-based text-sharing classroom provides for the opening up of ideas, the publication of student writing, and the promotion of the student as teacher, or what has been called here the "enfranchising" of the student.

CONCLUSION

In much the way that postmodern philosophers like Heidegger and Foucault developed their theories in reaction to the "modern" foundational philosophies that followed Kant, a postmodern pedagogy constitutes a reaction to the traditional practices of the writing classroom. Although change has occurred recently in composition pedagogy, including a much-heralded shift from a product to a process model, the writing student, as we have shown, remains locked into an instructional environment that seems oblivious to (1) the changing nature of the student population,

(2) a shifting base of economic support, (3) current emphases on social justice and ideological issues, and (4) the real-world purposes of writing itself.

Simply plugging computers into classrooms will not automatically transform this instructional environment. Nothing has proven more dismal than the lack of instructional success microcomputers have demonstrated in their brief careers as drill-and-practice machines, pseudo-human tutors, and automated graders. But computers do provide us the opportunity to view the instructional process in entirely new ways. As Papert describes them, computers are in and of themselves heuristic devices, for "they have catalyzed the emergence of ideas" (p. 186).

But if a postmodern pedagogy is a reaction to an unsatisfactory status quo, then that status quo must be described as processes that a postmodern pedagogy can amend or transform. This we have done by describing the liabilities of instructor feedback and the proscenium classroom itself, the false nature of the audience imposed on the student writer, and the difficulties and inefficiencies in trying to adapt current-traditional methods to transactional or group work. We have shown how network theory, or a new model of classroom interaction based on networked computers, empowers the student writer and deneutralizes his sense of text. Further, we have shown that network theory rejects elitist epistemologies that support an "information transfusion" or teacher-centered model of instruction in favor of social constructivist models that privilege a communal process of knowledge making. These social-constructionist models, implemented through the computer-based collaborative approach and specifically employing psychological filtering, encourage the open expression of diversity and the active participation of all students.

It is relatively easy to make utopian pronouncements concerning the computer and its effects on classroom instruction. It is also, we have discovered, easy to confound the real benefits of using computers by pasting computer processes on outmoded paradigms of instruction. Whatever uses the computer will be put to in the writing classroom, the effectiveness of such uses will depend more on a controlling pedagogy and its theoretical base than on the technical capabilities of the machines themselves.

WORKS CITED

Benveniste, Guy. "New Politics of Higher Education: Hidden and Complex." *Higher Education* 14 (1985): 175–195.

Berlin, James. "Rhetoric and Ideology in the Writing Class." *College English* 50 (September 1988): 477–494.

Britton, James, et al. *The Development of Writing Abilities (11–18)*. Schools Council Research Studies. London: Macmillan, 1975.

Bruffee, Kenneth. "Social Construction, Language, and the Authority of Knowledge: A Biographical Essay." *College English* 48 (1986): 773–790.

Foster, David. *A Primer for Writing Teachers: Theories, Theorists, Issues, Problems.* Portsmouth, NH: Boynton/Cook, 1983.

Gere, Anne Ruggles. *Writing Groups: History, Theory, and Implications.* Published for the Conference on College Composition and Communication. Carbondale: Southern Illinois, 1987.

Hairston, Maxine. "The Winds of Change: Thomas Kuhn and the Revolution in the Teaching of Writing." *College Composition and Communication* 33 (February 1982): 76–88.

Hoy, David Couzens. "Foucault: Modern or Postmodern?" *After Foucault: Humanistic Knowledge, Postmodern Challenges.* Ed. Jonathan Arac. New Brunswick, NJ: Rutgers, 1988, pp.12–41.

Johnson, David W., et al. "Effects of Cooperative, Competitive and Individualistic Goal Structures on Achievement: A Meta-Analysis." *Psychological Bulletin* 89 (1981): 47–62.

LeFevre, Karen Burke. *Invention as a Social Act.* Published for the Conference on College Composition and Communication. Carbondale: Southern Illinois, 1987.

Mingle, James R. *Challenges of Retrenchment.* San Francisco: Jossey-Bass, 1981.

Norris, Christopher. *Contest of Faculties: Philosophy and Theory after Deconstruction.* London: Methuen, 1985.

Ong, Walter J. "Literacy and Orality in Our Times." *The Writing Teacher's Sourcebook.* Ed. Gary Tate and Edward P. J. Corbett. New York: Oxford, 1981, 1988, pp. 37–46.

Papert, Seymour. *Mindstorms: Children, Computers, and Powerful Ideas.* New York: Basic Books, 1980.

Riesman, D. *On Higher Education: The Academic Enterprise in an Era of Rising Student Consumerism.* San Francisco: Jossey-Bass, 1980.

Rorty, Richard. *Philosophy and the Mirror of Nature.* Princeton, NJ: Princeton, 1979.

Sharan, Shlomo. "Cooperative Learning in Small Groups: Recent Methods and Effects on Achievement, Attitudes, and Ethnic Relations." *Review of Educational Research* 50 (1980): 241–271.

Shor, Ira. *Critical Teaching and Everyday Life.* Boston: South End Press, 1980.

Townsend, R. C. "Training Teachers for an Open Classroom." *College English* 31 (1970): 710–724.

Minimalism, Populism, and Attitude Transformation: Approaches to Teaching Writing in Computer Classrooms

ERIC JAMES SCHROEDER
University of California, Davis
JOHN BOE
University of California, Davis

We'd rather teach writing in a computer classroom than in a regular classroom. Computer classrooms make teaching writing simpler; such classes can be more easily focused on writing and are usually more enjoyable. But we can imagine, indeed have visited, computer classrooms where the technology distracts from the real subject matter (writing), commanding large amounts of time and energy.

Our approach toward the technology is minimalist: We believe classroom goals should dictate hardware and software purchases. In other words, writing programs that want to use computers as word processors and nothing else don't need Mac II's or IBM O/S 2's. Likewise, programs more interested in the *writing* process than in word-processing gimmicks require only low-end word-processing software like WriteNow, not Microsoft Word 4.0. Above all, pedagogical goals—not budget or belief in the ultimate virtue of technology—should shape hardware and software decisions.

We argue for a minimalist approach because we believe the proliferation of computers should be a populist rather than an elitist movement. Writing is an activity that every college student engages in. (Indeed, UC Berkeley Professor Donald McQuade recently asserted to one of us that writing was the most significant activity college students engage in regularly.) Since we believe word processors can make the writing process easier and more efficient (and, in some cases, make the product better as well), colleges and universities should strive to make this technology accessible to all their students. We are dismayed that some colleges rank computer tasks in order of perceived importance, with word processing generally given low priority. We find such rankings particularly ironic since college surveys show word processing as the primary computer activity. If most people want to use computers for word processing, then word processing is the most important use for computers.

Because we indeed believe computers can make writing easier and, we hope, help improve it, our goal in using them is to modify students' attitudes toward writing, and thus their writing behavior. We believe computers can help us change the way students view writing as well as change their actual writing process. We believe computers can alleviate some anxiety about writing, thus making students more confident writers. Furthermore, computers can make them more knowledgeable about the writing process, more able to use prewriting and revision strategies.

MINIMALISM

When we began using computers to teach composition, we made two conscious decisions: (1) We wanted to use computers in the context of a classroom rather than a lab, and (2) we wanted this room to be user friendly. In short, we wanted writing to be fun (or at least more fun). We knew what we didn't want: Ours was a minicomputer campus using the UNIX operating system, and many of us had had our fill of UNIX's power and complexity. So had our students.

We decided a minimalist approach was in order. The year before, we'd finished a study (Stenzel et al. 1989) that showed what

everybody else was learning too: Word processing doesn't necessarily improve student writing. This finding was no surprise given
the UNIX system, but the study also recommended that administrators who design computer facilities should think about not
only the kinds of computers and operating systems available, but
also about the writing environment itself. Our first decision—what
computer to use—was easy. Our computer center had Macintoshes
available, and it didn't take us long to recognize the minimalist
virtues of the machine.

First, the Mac is small: 13.6 in. x 9.6 in. x 10.9 in. (9.5 kg.).
Because we were interested in a classroom rather than a lab environment, we wanted machines that students could see over and
around, that wouldn't get in the way of their interaction with each
other and with the teacher. The bigger the computer, the more it
commands the students' attention. Similarly, the noisier the computer, the more it commands the students' attention: the Mac Plus
is not only small, it's silent.

Second, the icon-based operating system is designed so even
an idiot (or even a long-time college composition teacher) can use
it. Since we began staff training with eight instructors, four of
whom had never touched the machine, we wanted software with a
minimal learning curve. As writing teachers, we didn't want to
waste our time teaching computer skills. Working on a 10-week
quarter system, we don't have time for that. (In the UNIX study,
students reported that on the average it took them seven weeks
before they felt comfortable with the machine.) We also soon
realized that we need teach only a minimal amount of the Mac
operating system in order for students to use it to perform basic
computer functions. We don't need to take class time to teach the
students about viewing files in different formats, sizing and moving windows, and so forth. Students will usually learn these tricks
on their own time anyway.

We also took a minimalist approach to software. After reviewing a variety of programs—word processors, style checkers,
outliners—we settled on the simplest, cheapest, most available
word processor, MacWrite. Nothing else. We wanted to teach students word processing during the first week of classes while still
introducing our curriculum, thus focusing the courses on composi-

tion rather than on computers. Even with MacWrite, we figured we wouldn't have to teach our students (or our fellow instructors) the whole program. (We have recently changed word processors—we now use WriteNow—which, with the upgrade of MacWrite to MacWrite 5.0 seems to be the best *low-end* word processor available.)

We wanted to focus on the traditional tasks involved in teaching writing, allowing experienced teachers to adapt the machines to their own classroom methods, strategies, and content. We also wanted to keep the focus on writing, to make the computer as inconspicuously simple as a pen and paper. No need for lengthy, confusing manuals. (In fact, we ended up writing our own minimalist manual, which sells for $1.58 in the college bookstore.)

Some administrators and teachers might ask, "With so much minimalism, why bother with computers at all? Is the investment in time and money in a computer classroom worth it if all you're going to do is word process?" Always eager to sell newer, more complex, and more expensive computers and programs, Apple Computer Inc. does seem to feel this way. One of their brochures explicitly states that computers should have loftier uses than "wimpy little tasks like one-page essays." If Montaigne had had this kind of computer and believed the brochure, he probably would have been an accountant rather than an essayist. We believe in the importance of writing—good old traditional writing. And computers can make performing *all* writing tasks more efficient.

The benefits that both students and teachers stand to reap are worth the energies and money invested in computer classrooms. But because minimalism *isn't* equivalent to cost cutting, minimal requirements for a classroom-based computer writing program are nonetheless substantial. Thus it is crucial that *each* student have a computer; the sharing of machines should occur as an optional, planned activity, not as a necessity. It is not, however, crucial that a program invest in high-end workstations (unless instructors have some nontraditional writing class activity in mind, which will require increased computing power). We must remember, too, that the larger the computer, the more its very size will likely command student attention, shifting the classroom focus from the community of writers to the monolithic technology.

Peripheral devices—printers, hard disks, modems—and such add-ons as memory expansion kits should be chosen primarily to complement classroom goals and to render the technology more transparent, less intrusive. For instance, the room should contain a sufficient number of printers so that students have fast access to hard copy when they need it. Most writers (and probably all newcomers to writing via computer) find editing easier and more efficient when they're working from the printed page rather than on the screen. They can see more text at a time, and the printed page is easier to read than the computer screen. (Although future writers may write and read only on computers, almost all present-day writers still regularly use hard copy as well.) Thus hardware requirement here is dictated by the very specific need for students to have immediate access to hard copy. From this need, though, how does an instructor arrive at the type and number of printers to use? That depends on how much printing will go on in the classes and what the instructor defines as "immediate access." For instance, a room in which every two machines share a dot-matrix printer seems like a good solution since it allows quick access for most printing needs. This arrangement causes other problems, however. Dot-matrix printers are often very noisy and, with heavy use, are susceptible to paper jams. Laser printers, although more costly (and seemingly antiminimalist), are faster and have fewer maintenance problems. (Obviously, they also produce more "beautiful" output, but for our pedagogical ends this is icing rather than cake.)

The decision to use any piece of hardware or software in the classroom should always be organic: An instructor must consider a particular innovation's impact on the whole set-up. Often, more expensive hardware—hard disk drives or laser printers—can simplify the classroom's operation. But the opposite is often true of software. Fancy programs generally have large learning curves, and they may be much more than instructors need to accomplish a particular task. (We still advocate pens and pencils for many writing tasks.) And because software can, in fact, end up costing more money than hardware, instructors should first know what tasks they want students to perform, then begin evaluating what's available. (Word-processing programs alone can range in price from $39 per copy to $495; more expensive is not necessarily better here.) Do students really need a fancy spell-checker that costs $99 per copy? If the program is difficult or time-consuming to operate, a $3.95 dictionary might be just as efficient (and maybe more so). Although instructors *might* want Microsoft Word 4.0 in order to teach technical writing or report writing, a basic word processor like WriteNow will do just fine for most freshman English classes. Spending a lot of money on software (or hardware) leaves less money to make computers and basic software available to increasing numbers of students and teachers. Simple economics combined with a populist point of view (computers for the people) dictate a minimalist approach.

There are two further minimal requirements if the goal is a writing classroom, rather than simply a writing lab. It's essential to have a *quality* projection device that allows students to see what's on the teacher's screen. The newer generations of such projection devices allow the lights to remain on, providing the teacher with an electronic blackboard that combines the best of computer and traditional classrooms. Additionally, computerized writing classrooms need some sort of networking hardware and software, to allow sharing of printers and, more importantly, sharing of texts (via a file server). (More later on projectors and file servers.)

POPULISM

Our populist pedagogical approach, based on the needs of the people actually involved in education (the students and the teachers), focuses on an overall goal of creating not a computer community, but a writing community. To create this writing community we must (1) make the technology widely available, (2) develop a sense of community that extends beyond the classroom, and (3) provide writing tasks that mimic real-world writing situations.

We have tried to make computer technology available to everyone, despite limited resources. In our case, we started with one computer classroom that serves approximately 14 sections of composition per quarter in a program that has nearly a hundred total sections per quarter. Two years later we added a second classroom. But whereas our long-term goal is to continue adding more facilities, we have in the meantime made accessible to all instructors a portable computer and projector; thus our instructors (those who had already developed innovative methods for teaching in the computer classroom) can turn a regular classroom into a computer classroom and so use their new ideas. In other words, if we can't bring students to the computer, we bring a computer to the students. One benefit of this portable set-up is that instructors unfamiliar with this new technology can get a chance to test it and decide whether they want to incorporate it into their teaching. Even in a one-hour class, students can quickly see the advantages of using computers for writing, and those who don't already use computers may be motivated to learn. Over time, instructors using portable computers can model writing behavior and techniques that students may learn to copy. The "portamac" thus becomes a way to extend the computer writing community into the traditional classroom.

In working to develop a sense of community within the computer classroom, we find that we borrow techniques and strategies from our traditional classes, then adapt and refine them. Just as they do in noncomputer classes, for instance, our students engage in a substantial amount of small-group work. And the computer can actually be used as a tool to bond small groups. On the first day of class, we begin by spreading the experienced computer users around—we encourage them to tutor students new to the computer and struggling with the technology. In doing so, we point out that the classmates they are helping may turn out to be good writers and return the favor in small-group edit sessions later in the quarter. Experience indeed shows such reciprocation happens quite often. Students quickly realize that different people have different expertise, and that through cooperating and sharing skill, more learning can take place.

Such a communal style of learning is sometimes necessitated when the instructor turns out to be a relative newcomer to the technology and a number of students know more about the computer than the instructor. (We've had instructors teaching computer sections who've only learned to use the computer the previous week, and of course we've had students who know a lot more about computers than even our most expert instructors.) Some instructors find this loss of authority unsettling at first, but quickly realize that it can have its advantages. When teachers recognize students' expertise, students are more likely to recognize and respect the teacher's expertise. One of the most dramatic ways of gaining this recognition is for teachers to share and analyze their own writing via the "electronic blackboard."

We also demonstrate our expertise by developing writing tasks that mimic real-world writing situations, which increasingly are computer writing situations. For instance, in one class we might model an assignment on the university's application form for its undergraduate research grants. The students would decide on a particular topic and then work in groups on different parts of the proposal, collaborating on the final product. After successfully completing the assignment, students who had an interest in doing so could then be encouraged to submit applications for projects they actually wished to pursue.

Our overall goal, then, has been to create a writing community made up of teachers, students, and administrators. And in dealing with each group, we have consciously tried to take a populist rather than an elitist approach.

First there is the community of teachers. In the past decade or so, we've all realized that teachers need to work with each other, sharing classroom experience and research formally and informally. The computer classroom with file server facilitates a new kind of conversation: easy sharing of exercises, assignments, sample student papers, even a place for dialogue between teachers. The models for this conversation haven't all been discovered; each community can create its own context, define its own pedagogy. For example, when we first set up our computer classroom, we soon realized that each instructor had developed or adapted for the computer unique and useful writing exercises. We set up a folder for such exercises on the instructors' hard disk. Although we believe teachers should give credit to others whose exercises they borrow (and offer a good example for the students' own borrowings), we must nonetheless set up a world where teachers can learn from each other, where, as the cliché goes, they need not reinvent the wheel. Our exercise folder has grown to such a size that we finally put together a manual of such exercises, together with strategies for teaching. We provide each computer classroom instructor with a copy of this manual and a disk copy as well. Thus teachers can easily borrow or adapt other teachers' exercises. (It's ironic that we encourage collaboration among our students but too often ignore it among ourselves.)

Teaching in a computer classroom, everyone seems to agree, minimizes the teacher's authority. It also saves time, because it's easier to teach in a computer classroom. There's no need to make photocopies; exercises or examples can be made by cutting and pasting from students' papers, which the teacher has on disk as well as in hard copy. For example, the teacher can cut and paste together a collection that includes the first paragraph (or first sentence) from each student's paper for a given assignment. Then, via the electronic blackboard, the class can discuss (and in some cases rewrite) these "openers." Such an exercise could, of course, be done in a conventional classroom (though without the dramatic modeling made possible with the electronic blackboard), but it would require someone typing up—or photocopying, then literally cutting and pasting—all the students' first paragraphs.

For most teachers, the focus of the course changes to take advantage of the way in which computers make rewriting easy. All of our instructors have their students spend less class time talking about essays in their books and more time writing about them. Furthermore, all instructors increased the amount of revision; indeed, some allow the students the option of rewriting all of their papers, an option, which, amazingly, some students take advantage of. (The problem of evaluating so many revisions is mitigated if the instructor gets them at the end of the term, when a holistic reading is appropriate.) The writing class becomes just that, a writing class.

The second community is the students. Obviously, the way teachers change their teaching affects the way students learn to write. They rewrite more, but they also write and rewrite more easily because not having to retype from drafts or earlier versions saves time.

Students also seem to enjoy the classes more. They like playing with their computers. (In the computer classroom, work often equals play.) The first year we were on line, the upper-division writing classes in our computer classroom had a 5 percent attrition rate compared with 17 percent for the whole program. Instructors also commented on less absenteeism. In our experience, part of the reason students like the classes is that they like the Macs. IBMs may still be the choice of Fortune 500 companies, but Macs are the overwhelming choice of teenagers. In many campus bookstores the Macs outsell the IBMs, sometimes by as much as 10 to 1. The university must, in computer choices as in much else, learn to listen to what students want and like.

Most students like writing on computers—any computers— just because they save time. And saving student time is in itself a positive good. Why should students have to spend time typing and retyping drafts? If, with their saved time, students work more on their classwork, wonderful. If they take this saved time and, instead of reading Schopenhauer, go to the beach or to a party, good for them. We want everyone, even students, to have free time. We believe student writing and student living will improve if we use computers to take some of the drudgery out of their writing tasks. We should rejoice in the existence of a technology that reduces some of the gratuitous pain built into American education.

The third community, the administrators, generally has the upper hand over the other two communities. Indeed, the problem often is making the administrative community respond to the real needs of the other two communities. Administrators need to be reminded that instructors and students—those who utilize the space—must have a voice in designing that space and selecting the appropriate technology for their ends.

Perhaps the central administrative problem with computer classrooms is that they take up sorely needed classroom space on most campuses. If administrators create computer classrooms, they have to be committed to getting maximum use out of the room. (Our first computer classroom handles more classes now than it did before we put computers into it.) With an ever-increasing need for more computer classrooms, administrators have to be creative in seeking out and utilizing space. For example, we helped solve the administrative problem of where to find space for a second computer classroom by housing the new classroom in the freshman dorms. This facility serves freshman composition and basic writing classes in which only dorm residents will be able to enroll. In the normal classrooms, students meet on our turf or neutral turf. This room is their turf. It's not a normal classroom; it's their living room. We expect that such a room will make students more comfortable with their composition classes. This new dorm classroom also doubles as a computer lab. There are other computer labs on campus, but to get to them dorm residents have to cross campus; to use them at night is especially a problem for women. Our new computer classroom/lab creates a real bedroom community; students can come down in their pj's and write.

In some respects money, though never unlimited, is less of a problem. After all, humanists (unlike our colleagues in the exact sciences) have never asked for large amounts of money for labs; it's hard for the authorities to turn down such first-time requests. The problem becomes deciding how to spend available funds. Software programs, especially those that go beyond word processing, can eat up money. Most sophisticated instructors who use computers have begun to realize the limitations of style-checking programs: They shift the audience from fellow human being to a machine that evaluates writing for "correctness." On the other hand, the latest entry in the software wars—hypertext programs— encourages using bigger, faster machines and seems to have enormous potential for disciplines that utilize an audio or visual medium or that use simulations. But those of us still teaching how to write plain old prose may not need or be ready for such programs—yet.

Not everyone has to have the latest technology. Super high tech is necessarily elitist. Often difficult to use and expensive to buy, such equipment necessarily can't be as available to everyone. If composition programs choose Sun workstations or Mac II's for word-processing labs (as some colleges have), these programs can't afford very many such machines or very many such labs.

Even when money is clearly limited, the temptation is often to buy the best technology, rather than to spread it to the most people. The higher up the administrator, the more likely he or she is to want to serve the stars on the faculties, to think of computers as tools for research rather than tools for teaching—to want to be at the cutting edge. Thus administrators who choose high-end workstations might find themselves unable to afford a machine for each student. We have seen such high-end classrooms; they are sometimes quite impressive, and they can yield interesting articles about the classroom of tomorrow, but they serve only a relative few of the students of today. Spending less money per machine, getting less state-of-the-art technology, lets one buy more machines. So we not only have a machine per student in our classroom, but also loaner machines to give to new instructors so they can take computers home. We also have more and more computer labs available so students can write on the machines at their convenience.

We like the Volkswagen or Model-T analogy: the Mac Plus is the people's machine because we can distribute it to more and more students who in turn can learn to drive it in a very short time. If we need to upgrade at some time in the future, we'll do so then. "One person—one computer" was Apple's motto in the early visionary Jobs/Wozniak days. This motto was "born of Jobs's conviction that the democratization of computer power would alter the balance between the individual and the institution" (Rose 1989). Of course, a *few* people need to be on the cutting edge in research and technology—and need the most expensive machines. But universities must remember their primary responsibility to teach the mass of their students.

ATTITUDE TRANSFORMATION

Computers change how we write and how we teach writing. But do computers improve student writing? To that end, each quarter we administer a questionnaire designed to measure the effectiveness of our program. We ask whether the students knew they were signing up for a computer class and whether they used these new skills in their other classes. We want to know this practical information, but we also want to start thinking about the larger question, that is, whether the computer changes the *quality* of their writing. Consequently, we ask students whether they feel the computer makes writing easier for them. The overwhelming majority tell us it does. This question sets them up for the kicker: Does using a computer *improve* their writing? A majority reply that yes, perhaps it improves their writing a bit. Although this information is obviously only anecdotal, we nonetheless find it significant. Even though we know that students, like everyone else, can have faulty perceptions of themselves, it's important to listen seriously to what they tell us.

It's also important to listen to what instructors say about computer use in their classes. In a recent survey we conducted, 8 out of 10 instructors who responded reported that the Macintosh changed the way they normally taught their courses. (One of the two who didn't change was a new instructor to the program.) The kinds of changes they listed included more collaborative work, more modeling, more time spent looking at student writing, more time spent doing exploratory writing. One instructor reported changing her role from teacher to consultant, and another confessed that he "found it difficult to be pretentious in a computer class." Furthermore, 8 out of 10 responded that they noticed a difference in their students' attitudes toward writing by the end of the quarter. Several said that their students wrote more drafts and revised more. One said her students experimented more, and another commented that her students not only had more fun, but also took writing more seriously. Most of these instructors also commented, however, that their students in noncomputer writing classes also experienced changes in their attitudes. A couple of them qualified this response, though, saying that the attitude shifts were different in the two groups. One instructor explained that the students in computer classes had a better attitude toward the writing *process*, whereas the noncomputer students were pleased that they were able by the end of the quarter to produce better *products*. To the final question—did the former students seem to improve more than the latter?—a majority of the respondents said that there was no difference between the groups, and one instructor thought her computer class improved much less. (She qualified this, though, by saying that the particular class was one of the worst she had ever taught.) Two instructors, however, thought their computer students improved a bit more, and two more instructors were outspoken in their belief that their Mac students improved much more; one of them claimed that "development of both sentence-level sophistication and overall essay organization improved dramatically for many students, from D- writing on the diagnostic essay to A-/B+ final exams."

Teachers, not computers, improve student writing, but computers make it easier for teachers to do so. Computers have indeed changed the way we and our students think about writing. Briefly, let us state the obvious: Drafting is easier, as is revising; we don't waste time retyping; there is less writer's block because it's obvious that the writing will be changed.

Collaboration is also much easier via computer, because both collaborators can write on the same text. We drafted this chapter together, then Eric took it home and rewrote it, then John took it home and rewrote it again. We sometimes used different fonts for our additions, so the partner could see what changes had been made most recently. Such collaborating works particularly well for us—we would argue that we probably couldn't collaborate if we didn't use the computer.

The real problem of such collaboration may be in the tendency to lose personal style: to write clearly but like a technician. Writing via committee becomes antiseptic and soulless, and even in collaboration with each other there is the danger of rejecting the personal and idiosyncratic in favor of the collective, the traditional, and the safe. What helps (for us, anyway) is the chance to integrate writing alone and writing together. When one of us has the text in his computer, it is his alone. Collaborative writing supplements but doesn't replace solitary creation.

Except for those few (usually older) people who cannot leave the "cherry orchard" of pen and paper, writing via computer is one of the few unambiguous technological advances of the postmodern (i.e., premillennial) era. For example, Gabriel Garcia Marquez, who, like most professional writers, writes almost every day, calls the word processor "the greatest discovery of my life." He used to average one finished page of copy per day, but, he says,

"Now I can do twenty, thirty, even forty pages a day! If I'd had this machine twenty years ago, I'd have published two or three times as many books" (Hamill 1988, p. 192).

We know from our own experience that although computers may not have improved our own writing, they have made us more productive. And quantity counts. Writing teachers are traditionally the most exploited and overworked class of college teachers. They can't afford the time to write and rewrite via typewriter. Computers make it possible for them to write (and a writing teacher should be a writer) as well as to fulfill their primary educational responsibilities.

With this ease of writing comes proliferating copy. Richard Lanham suggests that print will start flowing more freely in purely electronic form and books and papers will become out of date, like the acoustic piano in the age of the electronic keyboard (Lanham 1989, p. 270). But, of course, acoustic pianos continue to exist, and doubtless there will be a place for hard copy—if not always, then at least in the foreseeable future. Perhaps there might be a welcome decline in the mass-market ideology that so dominates current-day publishing; maybe, with computers, we can support *local* communities of writers and readers, and, with desktop publishing, even see our works on paper as well as on screen. In any event, if more people are writing more, then the available audience will inevitably be spread out thinner.

Part of the reason that many people (including us) are more productive using computers is that, finally, they are more fun to write on. Keyboarding does have a magical quality, making words, sentences, paragraphs appear and disappear at a stroke. The video display (which, like so many pleasurable things, may be hazardous to your health) certainly contributes to this sense of pleasure. For many, TV screens are associated with enjoyment; similarly, many have played computer games, and so again associate the computer with recreation. Perhaps these associations themselves help make writing more fun, less painful.

That writing on computers is more fun is, of course, obvious to students, but the primary factors that make *us* want to do our writing on computers aren't necessarily obvious to student writers. As writing teachers, therefore, we must model our own writing practices. We do this with a video projector (currently a liquid crystal display unit), which projects the small screen of the teacher's computer onto a large, overhead screen.

Having a projector in the room allows us to focus the class directly on the writing process. By having my screen projected in front of the class I can, in a way never before possible in writing classes, show the students how I write and rewrite. For example, I might show how I would rewrite a section from a student's paper. Of course, this kind of modeling is risky—what if I get stuck? What if I write an awkward sentence? What happens in these cases is usually that the class gets involved, starts offering corrections, improvements. Classroom writing thus becomes truly collaborative.

One of the most instructive stories about education comes from a friend who studied mathematics in graduate school. He had one professor who would present proofs on the board with unerring accuracy—really teaching, the friend assumed, how mathematics should be done. His other math professor would often get lost in the middle, have to erase a few steps and figure out where he went wrong, even have to ask his class for help. Sometimes he'd end the class without completing a proof. Initially the friend assumed the first teacher was the good one. But as he went on with his study, he realized that the second professor was showing him what doing math was really like. The first, with his always elegant, always perfect proofs was being a textbook, not a teacher. Using a projection device in a computer classroom, writing teachers can act like the second professor; by showing that writing is a messy (and recursive) process, they can liberate themselves and their students by modeling what writing is really like.

Such a classroom approach is necessarily improvisatory. Composition teachers should be used to this. A good metaphor for the teacher faced with a composition classroom hour is that of a writer facing the blank page. He may have certain plans, but he needs to improvise, to create, to trust to luck. One favorite activity in a traditional classroom is to distribute photocopies of a student paper and to respond to it. This activity—collaborative and unstructured, unsupported by notes—models the act of a writer rewriting, treats text as something that can be improved. In the traditional classroom, the teacher goes home, reads the papers, selects a few, photocopies them, then shares them with the class. In the computer classroom, however, the students hand in their papers over the electronic network (as well as, if desired, in hard copy), and the class can immediately start looking at them. Of course, the teacher hasn't had the advantage of being able to preselect appropriate papers, of having been able to figure out what to say about these papers. But in some ways this is all to the good. The teacher becomes, just like everyone else in the class, a reader/writer who has to respond to a new text. The talented teacher can then really model the process of reading and rewriting. And this modeling can, in turn, shape the students' writing behavior.

Most students write a draft and then try to fix their mistakes, giving their paper a cosmetic once-over. But if the teacher models how to use the computer in writing, students will become more inclined (or can be persuaded) to use the computer to do large-scale revisions. Since retyping is not involved, the teacher can more easily demand such substantive revisions. But students must be given class time to try out revision strategies for themselves, adopting the ones that work for them and discarding the ones that don't. They must also be given time to work with each other, discussing their own writing habits and learning too what works for their peers.

For the purpose of sharing texts and collaborating, a file server is essential. Having one in the room allows us to communicate more quickly and efficiently. At the most basic level, we're able to give students assignments, in-class exercises; they're able to give us their texts. But more exciting, they can give each other their texts—they can interact in a way impossible in a traditional classroom.

Having a file server to facilitate collaborative writing allows us to model how most writing is done in the real world. Collaborative writing isn't just another buzzword; increasingly the workplace relies on computer networks to facilitate collaboration. Collaborative writing takes place in all sorts of ways and in all sorts of work environments. In the classroom, we're limited only by our imaginations.

Furthermore, the computer enhances the possibility of writing for an audience. By putting copies of their drafts on the file server, students can readily get audience responses. As J. B. Yeats, the poet's father, said, "A work of art is the social act of a solitary man" (Ellman 1978, p. 17). The individual, even when writing in isolation, is always writing and rewriting for an audience, and the computer makes this audience more reachable. In the computer classroom, the duality between collaboration and individual creation is resolved by the audience—both teacher and fellow student—becoming collaborators. There's an audience available even at the draft stage; instead of "writer" versus "audience," everyone is part of the writing community, everyone is writer *and* audience.

In the future, even more radical collaboration is promised by the spread of hypertext and other technological advances, which have the potential to bridge the gap between audience and author even more. (See Moulthrop 1989; Lanham 1989.) Maybe we will find an audience for proliferating electronic copy by breaking down boundaries between audience and writer, by making reading interactive, by making the reader literally into the writer. We admire thinkers like Lanham and Moulthrop who bring their visionary outlook to literary studies. Yet composition teachers still must face the (perhaps) duller pedagogical necessity of working with the widely available technology of today.

In our program, three years old and growing, we are working to effect a dramatic change in students' attitudes toward writing. Our goal is not merely to improve their writing in 10 short weeks (how much, after all, can writing improve in 10 weeks?); rather, our goal is to change attitudes toward writing, to create attitudes that will allow students to keep improving their writing for the rest of their lives. The foremost change is making writing, if not more fun, certainly less painful. Perhaps our students will ultimately become more productive and, with hard work and good teaching, better writers.

Every year more writing and more teaching of writing is being done via computer. Our surveys show that most instructors, like most students, prefer such classrooms. We believe that whether individual composition instructors and administrators like it or not, by the twenty-first century all or almost all college writing classes will be held in computerized classrooms. We are actively proselytizing our colleagues in the University of California system and around the country, trying to get writing teachers and administrators to start examining the issues, to decide if they want a minimalist or a "maximalist" approach, a populist or an elitist approach, whether ultimately they are teaching students a fixed, canonical course content or whether they are trying to transform student writing behavior and give them skills that will last a lifetime.

WORKS CITED

Ellman, Richard. *Yeats: The Man and the Mask*. New York: Norton, 1978.

Hamill, Pete. "Love and Solitude." *Vanity Fair* 51, no. 3 (March 1988): 125–131, 192.

Lanham, Richard. "The Electronic Word: Literary Study and the Digital Revolution." *New Literary History* 20 (1989): 265–290.

Moulthrop, Stuart. "In the Zones." *Writing on the Edge* 1, no. 1 (Fall 1989): 18–27.

Rose, Frank. *West of Eden: The End of Innocence at Apple Computer*. New York: Viking, 1989. Quoted by Susan Kinsley in *The New York Times Book Review* (May 7, 1989): 14.

Stenzel, John, Linda Morris, and Wes Ingram. "The Effects of Minicomputer Text-Editing on Student Writing in Upper Division Cross-Disciplinary Courses: Results of a Study by the Writing Center, University of California, Davis." *Computers and Composition* 6, no. 2 (1989): 61–79.

Computers in the Classroom: The Instruction, the Mess, the Noise, the Writing

CAROLYN BOIARSKY
Illinois State University

My first job out of college was as an investigative reporter with United Press International (UPI). It was back in the early 1960s, just at the beginning of the War on Poverty, and I was dispatched to the front lines to cover the skirmishes taking place in the Appalachian Mountains.

Stationed in Charleston, West Virginia, I found the UPI office on the fourth floor of an old orange brick building at the edge of the downtown sector. The office was a single room, about half the size of a normal classroom, with six of us—the teletypesetter, the Bureau Chief, and four reporters—usually crammed into it. In the middle of the room, four very old, scarred and battered wooden desks were pushed together to form one large table, and the four of us, two on each side, sat facing each other, pounding ancient manual typewriters. At the far end of this makeshift conference table was a long, thin stand that held a dictionary, thesaurus, *UPI Style Guide,* and the West Virginia Blue Book, which contained everything anyone needed to know about politics in the Mountain State. Surrounding us on three sides, the teletype machines constantly clacked away as information came in over the wire. On the fourth side was the Bureau Chief's desk. It was pushed over to a corner of the room by a window overlooking the Kanawha River. The office was messy, noisy, constantly in motion. And I loved it. This is where I learned to write.

I quickly learned to filter out everything and everybody when I needed to concentrate on writing a story. But on the whole, writing became a social activity. If I needed to know whether to put a comma before *and* in a series, I simply asked whoever was sitting at the table. Someone usually knew. If no one remembered, Carlos, who liked to sit at the far end of the table, would check the rule out in the style guide. Since I was new to West Virginia, I was thin on background. Often, as I would be writing up a story, especially on Wednesdays when I was responsible for writing a political column for the Sunday papers, I'd need to know the history of an event. Most of the time one of the others sitting around the table could fill me in. Even if no one knew, someone could at least point me toward a good source.

I became adept at writing from different points of view. I had to meet two major deadlines, one for the morning and one for the evening papers, but I also had a deadline every two hours for the radio and TV wire. That meant that in an eight-hour shift I could conceivably write and rewrite the same story three or four times. I usually ran out of ideas for a new angle after the third time and passed the story on to someone else.

Reporters collaborate on a story.

Whatever I wrote could always be improved. Everything went to the Bureau Chief for editing before it was handed over to the teletypesetter to be put on the wire. Language could be sharpened, syntax made more concise, information expanded or deleted. It wasn't just my copy that got edited; it was everybody's, even the "old boys" who had been in the business for years.

That first experience as a professional writer, as I struggled to acquire skills that no English class had ever taught me, would have been much more difficult if it hadn't been for the understanding and support I received from the other writers seated around that oversized table. I was part of a community. We tried out our ideas on each other, helped each other come up with clever angles, and thought up punchy endings for each other's stories. I had help when I needed it, and, when my first piece was published in *The New Republic*, I had friends to celebrate with me. The drudgery, the isolation that is inevitably a part of writing, was diminished.

Today, with the help of the computer, my freshman composition class is beginning to resemble that newsroom bullpen. Student writers sit at their desks, surrounded by notes, typing their stories into their computers. Periodically, a student calls out a question in relation to the computer—"How do you get italics?"— or in relation to composing—"How do you spell *affiliate?*" And someone usually shouts back, "One L." In the background is the constant buzz of a printer as it churns out hard copies to be read over. At times students correct these immediately; at other times they collaborate with each other, seeking suggestions for improvement. A dictionary, thesaurus, and handbook lie on an empty workstation at the far end of the room for reference. Occasionally a student leaves class early to get more information.

I don't perceive those in my classroom as "students," but as young writers the way I was back in that UPI office. Nor do I perceive myself as a teacher, but rather as an editor. I, too, sit at a workstation. Periodically a student brings me some hard copy to look at. More often than not, the student beckons me over to the computer to take a look at a problem on the monitor. In the one networked class the student sends his or her piece directly to me. Either way, we two—the student and I—collaborate as writer and editor to identify problems and develop strategies for solving them. The room is messy, noisy, constantly in motion. And I love it. There is real writing going on. This is how I learned to write and this is how my students will learn to write.

ALTERING THE PHYSICAL SETTING

The computer, more than any staff development program, journal article, or administrative mandate, has the potential to alter the environment of the classroom, and with it the role of both teacher and student. A computerized classroom can blur the line between teacher and student and enhance students' active participation in their learning. Although a good teacher can create such a collaborative learning environment regardless of the classroom setting, certain configurations facilitate such an atmosphere.

The linear configuration (see Figure 3-1), which emulates the pattern of the traditional classroom, creates the least amount of change in student–teacher roles. Students sit in horizontal lines of workstations facing the teacher's desk, chalkboard and projection

Figure 3-1

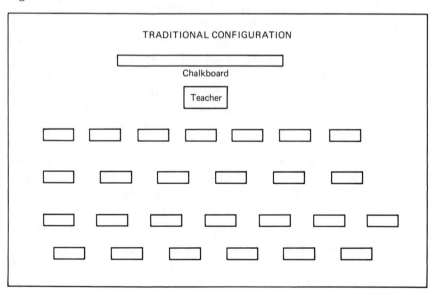

screen at the front of the room. A wide aisle like the DMZ separates students from teacher. The dynamics of the room are implicit. The teacher leads, actively providing information and relaying instructions while the students respond, passively receiving the data and carrying out the instructions. Interaction between teacher and students and among students is minimal. Aisles between the rows of workstations are too close to permit much movement, even to slip out for an emergency pit stop. Students' only opportunity to interact is with those on either side of them. Intercourse with those directly behind them is usually resorted to only in cases of extreme need since it requires some amount of physical dexterity.

A more flexible pattern, the elliptical configuration (see Figure 3-2) increases the potential for interaction among students. With workstations placed around the perimeter of the room, the open center becomes a common area for students to meet to discuss their papers. However, this configuration has its drawbacks. Students can feel isolated because they face the wall as they

Figure 3–2

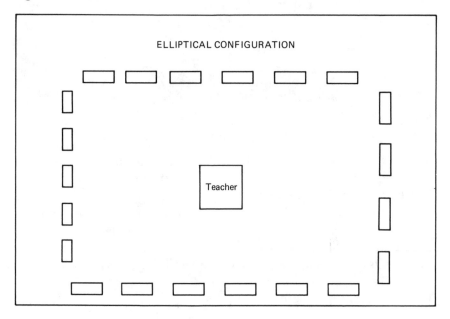

The elliptical configuration.

work. Their backs to each other and to the center of the room, they cannot make eye contact easily and often find themselves addressing the backs of people's heads.

Whereas this configuration doesn't do much to encourage interaction among the students, it does lessen the distance between them and the teacher. Rather than being located at the head of the class, a position that no longer exists with this architecture, the teacher's workstation is often located in the center of the room where students have easy access to her.

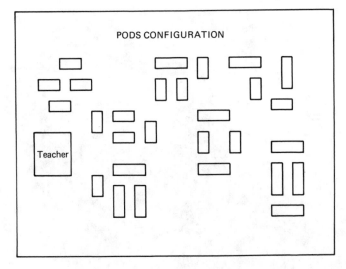

PODS CONFIGURATION

Teacher

Figure 3–3

The pods configuration (see Figure 3-3), a technological version of the UPI office, comes closest to the newsroom bullpen. Scattered throughout the room, the pods consist of clusters of four workstations with students facing inward toward each other. The teacher's workstation is located on the edge of one of these clusters, in a position similar to that of the UPI bureau chief's.

The pod architecture is by far the most preferable. Because students within each pod face each other, interaction is not only facilitated, but natural. Looking inward toward each other, students make eye contact easily, extending and accepting invitations for collaboration. The classroom itself appears fluid and dynamic, with room for students and teacher to move about, freely interacting with those in other pods. The line between teacher and students is further subverted as the teacher's workstation is integrated with the others, creating the impression that the teacher is also a writer.

Installing computers in a classroom usually requires some renovation in terms of wiring. It is not much more difficult to wire for a scattered pod configuration than it is for either the traditional linear or the increasingly common elliptical pattern. Depending on the size and shape of the room, it is possible to

Working in pods.

accommodate as many students in the pod configuration as in the others.

The introduction of computers provides an opportunity to alter the traditional physical arrangement of a classroom so that the entire environment becomes more conducive for young writers. What better arrangement than that of a true community of writers—a newsroom?

I recently visited the newsroom of the local newspaper, the *Peoria Journal Star*, which converted to computer technology about 10 years ago. Workstations were arranged in clusters of three, four, or five desks with the City Editor's desk located in one of the middle clusters. Reporters wandered about, discussing their stories by the coffeepot, checking a piece coming over the wire on the far side of the room, sharing information at another reporter's desk. Small, illegibly written notes with data, telephone numbers, and the names of sources sailed like paper airplanes back and forth across the workstations as newswriters tossed one another tidbits of information. Periodically, someone wandered over to the City Editor's desk for advice. More often than not, the City Editor left his own station, where he inevitably would be working on a story someone had sent over the network for editing, to check on something at a reporter's desk.

Despite the technological changes, the room didn't appear very different from pre-PC days, when we'd all used manual Smith Coronas. However, the designers who'd been brought in to plan the configuration for the new technology had originally tried to superimpose a business layout with partitions around each writer and a separate office for the City Editor. But the dynamics of a newsroom differ radically from those of a business. Reporters are social; they need to have access to each other. In addition, the City Editor needs to be available to the staff. The editor doesn't need a separate office or even a special chair, which the designers suggested after their idea for an office was scotched, to let people know who he is. Everyone who needs to know does.

Just as the needs of reporters have to be met, the social needs of student writers need to be met. And it is just as necessary for the teacher to be an integral part of her class as it is for the City Editor to be accessible to his staff.

TEACHER AS EDITOR

Whereas the linear configuration maintains the teacher's traditional role as leader and giver of information and the students' traditional role as receivers of knowledge, the elliptical and pod configurations necessitate new roles for teacher and students alike.

In these unique configurations there is no longer a "front" to the classroom. Students' eyes are drawn to a monitor rather than to a lectern or chalkboard. The traditional lecture format is no longer valid. The classroom inevitably becomes a workshop in which students, as young writers, learn to write by writing, acquiring skills as they write with the help of a teacher who now assumes the role of editor.

For teachers who have never worked closely with an editor in getting a story into print or who have failed to understand the relationship of Maxwell Perkins to the writings of Thomas Wolfe, the amount of help they provide their students in this role may at times appear excessive and prolonged. But it isn't; it's what every good editor provides authors.

In this new role as editor, the teacher becomes what Mortimer Adler in his *The Paideia Proposal* (1982) calls a coach: "A coach trains by helping the learner to *do*, to go through the right motions, and to organize a sequence of acts in a correct fashion" (p. 27). A baseball coach doesn't simply give a lecture on how to hold a bat; he helps the little leaguer to place his hands on the bat correctly. And not just the first time, but each time the child comes to bat, until the child gets it right. Like the baseball coach, we need to work one-on-one with students as they work on their texts. We need to continue to provide assistance until the students get it right, not give up after they fail on the first or even the second try after our lecture.

Editors—really good ones—work through a story with their writers. Whether they assign the story or simply approve the idea for one, they never send the writer off to compose until they have both collaborated on the angle the story might take, the informa-

Assistant city editor shares a story with a colleague in the newsroom.

tion required, and a possible pattern of organization. After they have looked at a draft, editors not only make suggestions for improvements, but often help the writer make those improvements.

The best editor I ever had was Nancy Smith during the one year she edited the *Atlanta Constitution Sunday Magazine*. A week after she returned an article to me for revision, I received a call from her. She was wondering how I was coming along—had I understood her comments, was I having any problems, and was there anything she could do to help? It was wonderful. Not only did she want my article, but she cared about *me*. She knew how demoralizing and frustrating revision could be, but she was there supporting me. I would have done anything for her. If she'd have told me to rewrite the whole damn thing, I'd have started over again without a murmur.

So now in my classroom I become Nancy Smith, roaming from workstation to workstation, offering help, giving support and backing away when students are hot, letting them run with the ball until they tire or become blocked. And the computer gives me the tools to work with. I suggest to a student whose text is jumpy, because he has used an AB/AB/AB pattern in writing a comparison/contrast, that he reorganize the information into an AAA/BBB pattern. Using the "copy" and "move" commands, he quickly and easily alters his text to fit the newly suggested pattern, still retaining the old version. Then he prints out both and together we determine which "sounds" better. In the same way, I help a student who isn't sure whether to include certain information in her paper. Using the "copy" and "delete" commands, she prints one copy of the text with the material and one without. Then we read over the two versions to decide whether the information is necessary for the reader's comprehension. When I see a student struggling over a transition sentence, I insert one with a few keystrokes, and when I find a student's text would flow better if he combined several sentences, I easily change the text to demonstrate my point.

I tread a fine line between giving students the answers and helping them learn to find those answers themselves. By suggesting a new organizational pattern, I provide the scaffolding to support them as they gain new insights and test out new skills in composing. The student must still put the information together, develop the transitions between the newly organized paragraphs, and ultimately decide which of the two patterns is the more effective. In the process, he finally understands firsthand the alternative organizational patterns for writing a comparison/contrast, which I introduced in a previous lecture and demonstration.

Trent Batson (Malarkey 1987) found that if students "spend three hours a week in a class where they write with a teacher skilled in maintaining topics and where they can 'scaffold' their writing . . . they have a chance to start improving. . . . Most importantly they write at higher levels than they are accustomed to, which builds confidence and expectations" (p. D-5).

With the following anecdote of a mother truly using scaffolding with her preschool child, Susan Florio-Ruane (1987) dispels the myth that teachers have always provided such support. When the child says "Da," the mother responds by clapping her hands, smiling, and telling her child in warm and excited tones, "That's wonderful. Yes, that's *Daddy*." She never says "No, it's not *Da*." Yet as teachers we consistently tell the child he's wrong and wait for him to give us the correct answer, afraid that if we give it to him we'll be "giving him the answers." But it's the mother's encouragement, coupled with the repetition of the correct pronunciation of "Daddy," that provides the child with the model that he imitates and finally emulates correctly.

Once during a workshop a teacher asked me when she could stop editing students' papers, when she would finally receive "finished" work. My answer was "Never." I have been freelancing for 20 years, but I can't think of anything I have ever handed in for publication that has not been improved by the revisions of a skilled editor.

Not too long ago I was struggling with the introduction to an article I was writing for the Sunday magazine of a large city newspaper. I was writing it from a first-person point of view, and, no matter what I did, it sounded like something out of a true confessions magazine. The pile of crumpled attempts filling the wastebasket under my desk was spilling onto the floor. The deadline, circled in red on the calendar hanging above my desk, had taken on the appearance of a neon sign. I was stuck. I couldn't move beyond the first paragraph when a member of the newspaper staff happened to call that day. I poured out my frustrations. To my relief, in a matter of minutes he had solved my problem. Only another writer, one who had grappled with the problem himself, could have given me that solution. It hadn't been something I could find in a grammar handbook; it was a writer's gimmick.

(Before the present article was ever sent to the editor, it was reviewed by two associates, one a senior partner in an editorial consulting firm, the other an educator. The reader has these reviewers to thank for reducing an overabundance of semicolons and eliminating a plethora of sentences beginning with *And* as well as reorganizing some fairly awkward sentences.)

But teachers don't have to be professional writers to help students acquire these skills. All of us have more writing experiences than our students. We have gained insights into communicating our thoughts to readers, and we can pass these on. So I become my students' editor. I show them how to improve their work and how their work improves with certain changes.

STUDENTS' CHANGING ROLES

Students, too, assume different roles in this newly configured writing community. They change from being passive recipients of a teacher's judgment to active seekers of constructive criticism. They give and receive assistance in the same way professional writers request and provide feedback in their own community. In contrast to the traditional classroom where students have no power and no authority, and are expected to be passive, in the pod configuration they assume authority as readers, becoming active learners seeking solutions to their problems. They assume responsibility not only for their own writing, but for each other's. They recognize that they need to spend time on each other's texts and provide each other with substantive suggestions; comments like "It sounds good to me" just don't cut it any more.

Becoming critical readers, they help each other improve their writing long before a teacher looks at it. As readers who are looking at a text in terms of content, they are capable of recognizing that a point in a text is confusing or contradicts some previous information, or that there is not sufficient information to support an assertion. In addition, they become proofreaders, marking and correcting mechanical errors in each other's texts while simultaneously instructing each other in the various rules involved. Usually at least one student in a group is fairly good at spelling, another good at punctuation, and a third knowledgeable in grammar.

By working in groups, they supplement each other's knowledge, and by providing each other with assistance, they free the teacher to spend time providing instruction that only she, with her knowledge and experience, can offer. As they begin to acquire new skills in writing as well as in such related areas as close reading, critical assessment, and problem solving, they become increasingly adept at helping each other.

When I was teaching at Georgia Tech, I had a second-semester composition class composed completely of jocks. The teams were always assigned priority in registration and tended to enroll in blocks. I had half the football team, two basketball players, half the girls' tennis team, and two poor souls whom the computer had somehow slipped onto the rolls. Known as scholar-athletes, my students demythologized the old axiom about athletes being all brawn and no brains. However, whereas they were completely assured of themselves on the playing field, they were fairly timorous in the classroom. Toward the end of the term, one of the six-footers came up to me with the typical boyish grin of a rural Georgia student. Shuffling in some embarrassment, he pointed toward a short, stocky student who two years later was to become the Yellow Jackets' leading player, and explained that John had told him to move the last paragraph up to the front of the text. He wanted to know what I thought of the idea. Only too willing to reinforce what experience had taught me was very often a valid response, I quickly scanned the paper and nodded in agreement. My jock-reader proudly squared a pair of shoulders that were already broad without artificial pads, and my six-foot writer, shaking his head in disbelief at his teammate's knowledge, returned to his seat to make the corrections.

I have found this pattern—a student-reader makes a suggestion to a student-writer who at first doesn't trust the other student's judgment—repeated over and over in class after class. Slowly students begin to gain confidence in their own and in each other's judgment as they find their suggestions echoed by the teacher. They also discover which students provide them with help in organization, which are good proofreaders, and which recognize flaws in content. For many students this role is antithetical to what has been ingrained in them since preschool. Previously they were taught not to talk to or get help from their peers, to stay in their seats, to raise their hands and wait for the teacher's help. In their new role, they not only may, but must, move out of their seats, talk to their peers, and even call out to the entire class. In addition, they discover they must cooperate rather than compete with one another. Many have been competing for grades since pre-

Students prepare to collaborate at the monitor.

school when mother compared them to Jane down the street. They have been told not to let others look at their papers, that it is wrong to give others the answers. Now they are, in effect, giving Jane the answers. And, finally, they have always perceived the teacher as the sole authority, the only one who knows the answers. Now they are learning that their classmates know answers, too.

We need to help them assume this new role, to provide them with an understanding of why they are assuming it, and then we need to teach them the necessary skills. If we don't, the results of this collaborative classroom will be similar to those of Freedman's study (1987). She found students circumventing the conferencing process, providing responses according to what they thought the teacher wanted rather than according to need, and failing to engage in real problem-solving activities.

How can we create a newsroom-style environment, and how can we help students adapt to it?

FOSTERING A NEWSROOM-STYLE ENVIRONMENT

Certainly the pod or even the elliptical configuration contributes much toward creating such an environment. However, even in the traditional linear classroom configuration, we can produce this environment. It simply takes more work.

The room should be furnished to meet a writer's needs. Just as the dictionary, thesaurus, style guide, and reference books were staples in the UPI office, they should be on hand to serve as references in the classroom. A book on writing research papers, perhaps a copy of *Bartlett's Quotations*, as well as a computer manual, should also be available along with copies of *The Atlantic Monthly, The New Republic*, and columns by Ellen Goodman and George Will to provide models of the types of writing in which students are engaged. An extra chair at the teacher's station can provide comfort for teacher and student, editor and writer, to confer.

But we need to go beyond these changes by creating an atmosphere of openness, informality, and conviviality. Such an atmosphere contributes much toward truly fostering an editor–

writer relationship between teacher and students as well as a peer system in which students rely on one another. I begin establishing this type of environment from the first day of classes. To accelerate the bonding process, I have the students swap their names, telephone numbers, and addresses with each other. Stressing the need for good attendance, since much of the course will involve group work, I encourage them to contact these group members if they are absent rather than ask me, "Did I miss anything important?" Thus, I begin to wean them from dependence on me as the sole authority and encourage them to seek each other for assistance instead.

The first writing assignment in which I engage my students further contributes to this bonding process by introducing them to collaborative writing in the following nonthreatening (read "nongraded") activity. After instructing students in the basic commands for using the computer and the word-processing program to provide basic skills for those who have never used the program and a review for those who have, I divide the students into pairs or trios. I give each group a computer function with which they are probably unfamiliar (justifying, using tabs, changing margins). Their assignment is to draft a set of directions for engaging in these functions. I don't tell them how to engage in them, but leave this for them to discover, forcing them to become actively involved in obtaining information. Once they have written the directions, the groups (1) swap texts, (2) perform a beta test (test out the directions on their computers, noting any problems), (3) give the papers back to the authors, (4) revise the directions based on the problems noted in the beta test, (5) conduct a second beta test, (6) engage in revisions where necessary, and finally (7) duplicate the directions for dissemination to class members. This realistic exercise demonstrates how collaboration in the planning, drafting, and revision phases of the writing process produces a truly effective product. In addition, the exercise introduces students to writing for a reader, as well as to the concept of revising to *improve* a text for the *reader's* sake rather than simply to correct it for a higher grade.

During this activity, I continue encouraging students to turn to each other for assistance. Invariably they will ask for my help with the first computer problem they encounter. Instead of providing them with the answer, I suggest that they check with the person on either side of them. If after checking they still don't have an answer, I either send them to someone in the class who knows the answer or I address the question to the class in general. If at that point no one knows, I send them to the reference table to look up the answer in the computer manual. I respond similarly to questions concerning composing. Thus, I am establishing a model of classroom behavior that includes moving about, calling out, and sharing information. And as I do so, I explain that I am teaching them not only to write, but to help each other write because "you can't take me with you." They can't take me to their history class when they have a report due or to their first job when they have to write a memo. Throughout the term I continue this process, requiring students to obtain help from each other and providing them with assistance only when I know their peers do not possess the necessary knowledge or skills to solve the problem.

This workshop-style environment necessitates a change in the format of a class. Little time is devoted to lectures. Instead, the course assumes the format of a workshop, with students engaging in the writing process during class when they can get help from each other and from the teacher. The process becomes intrinsic to the students, who plan, draft, revise, and proofread in the same way professional writers do. Only after the first assignment is completed does the instructor need to offer a brief lecture on the process, emphasizing metacognition, allowing the students to think about how they wrote their paper. And then the class moves to the next assignment—learning to write by writing—with the teacher-editor providing a scaffold on which students can climb to gain skills in planning and revising the way a good editor nurtures writers.

Under this new format, conferencing occurs during class time. No longer are there long lines snaking around a hallway outside an instructor's office as students slouch against walls waiting to discuss their plans or drafts. Instead, teacher and students engage in numerous discussions throughout the class periods. Nor do teachers have to wait until students turn in a paper to discover they are going in the wrong direction. By scanning students' texts on their monitors, teachers can "head them off at the pass."

I help students acquire skills in composing through their own writing rather than through lectures or exercises. I no longer "call the shots," determining what topics will be learned today, tomorrow, and next week, but rather teach as the need arises for each student-writer. Like Nancie Atwell's curriculum (1987), mine "unfolds."

I provide instruction not only in composing, but also in responding critically to a text. Students are usually reluctant to be too critical about each other's work, though they realize they need someone to help them with their own texts. One way for students to overcome this double-edged problem is to openly elicit relevant criticism from their peers. However, often they don't know what help is really needed or they can't articulate their problem. Nancy Sommers (1981) comments that students often "feel" that something is wrong with their text, but they don't know what it is. As I work with the students, I help them learn to analyze these feelings in relation to what they know about rhetoric, and I provide them with a basic vocabulary related to composing so that they can verbalize their feelings. Using professional terminology, I discuss with them my analysis of their problems and my strategies for solving them. I may read through a student's text and comment that the paper doesn't seem to have a single idea, that there seem to be several ideas and I don't see their relationship to one another; there just doesn't seem to be a *focus*. However, the first sentence of the last paragraph suddenly makes everything in the paper clear. Because it provides the framework for perceiving the relationship among the various ideas, it provides the *organizing idea* for the text. The student usually responds with a tentative suggestion, often couched as a question, wondering whether he should use that sentence to introduce the text rather than to conclude with it. Soon, like the Georgia Tech jock, he is recognizing similar problems in others' papers and he can provide the others with a relevant analysis rather than simply comment that "something's missing."

To provide a structure in which students can respond effectively to each other's text, I divide their revision activities into four stages. During the first stage students respond solely to the writer's content, using reader protocol activities similar to those de-

The instructor works along with students at his own PC in a pod.

veloped at Carnegie Mellon University (Schriver 1984). In the second phase students concentrate on such areas as coherence and reader interest. Next they work on readability—syntax and language. Just before they turn in their papers, they engage in the final stage of proofreading—grammar, usage, punctuation, and spelling. By structuring these peer-response sessions, I lead students into providing each other with specific feedback for a text. Slowly they begin to internalize these steps. As the term progresses, they turn more and more to each other for help. And, as my jock class demonstrated, when they hear their opinions validated by me, they begin developing confidence in each other's assistance.

As for my relationship with them, I purposely integrate my own writing and composing activities into the class. They begin to perceive me as a writer, not just a teacher. By writing along with them and reading my writing aloud when it isn't very good, by showing them my early drafts when the writing is disorganized and going nowhere, I become less intimidating. By talking to the computer when I have difficulty with it, going so far as to use an expletive when the machine threatens to gain mastery, I become more like them. They relate to me as a writer who experiences the same problems and the same frustrations they have rather than as an authority figure with the "right" answers.

With this perception, the classroom begins to be transformed into my old UPI newsroom. Messy. Noisy. Constantly in motion. My students are becoming writers. I have become their Bureau Chief. And I love it. We have truly become a community of writers.

WORKS CITED

Adler, Mortimer. *The Paideia Proposal*. New York: Macmillan, 1982.

Atwell, Nancie. *In the Middle: Writing, Reading, and Learning with Adolescents*. Portsmouth, NH: Boynton/Cook, 1987.

Florio-Ruane, Susan. "The Classroom Context." Presentation for "Contexts for Teaching Writing" Conference, April 26, 1987.

Freedman, Sarah Warshauer. *Response to Student Writing*. Urbana: National Council of Teachers of English, 1987.

Malarkey, Tucker. "English the Write Way." *The Washington Post* (May 5, 1987): D-5.

Schriver, Karen A. "Revising Computer Documentation for Comprehension: Ten Exercises in Protocol-Aided Revision." Pittsburgh: Carnegie-Mellon, Communications Design Center, 1984.

Sommers, Nancy. Presentation at the Conference on College Composition and Communication, Dallas, 1981.

The Computer Classroom and Collaborative Learning: The Impact on Student Writers

CAROL KLIMICK CYGANOWSKI
DePaul University

Collaboration in using computers and in writing can create a student-centered, cooperative community in the writing classroom and beyond. From its integration in writing classes, the computer lab often becomes a physical center for a student writers' community—a place to meet partners in collaborative projects, to find willing readers, to write along with other writers.

Using standard word-processing software along with collaborative classroom techniques provides opportunity for students to collaborate, while encouraging innovation—both in writing and in discovering new ways to use word processing to enhance their own and their partners' writing processes. Employing collaborative invention and revision techniques that stimulate students to interact with each other, to "play" with the software, and to practice word-processing functions (like Block and Move) that aid and encourage macro-level revisions changes how students view readers and the writing process and changes the kind of revisions students habitually use. More than half the papers in collaborative computer sections show students moving blocks of text within a paper.

When students use computers to collaborate in invention, revision, and editing, the immediacy and physical connection of the computer lab enhances peer response and creative collaboration. The computer monitor's suitability to sharing writing along with word processing's ability to display readable copy throughout any number of changes encourages students to make their writing available to readers and to make readers' responses part of their composing and revising process. Linking reading and talking about writing to trying alternatives essentially erases the negative factor of students' feeling their work is "cut up" by others. Using word-processing functions to rearrange and reinvent (while retaining the original text in separate files), students create new plans and parts as they respond to each other's writing. Word processing's facility in developing and storing multiple versions of a text invites students to view the computer lab as a place for sharing and trying. Keyboarding and disk storage of multiple files eliminate the need for additional procedures or devices to record group work.

As students become agile in maximizing the benefits of word processing and collaboration, add-on applications programs become useful parts of the writing process. Commercial software that automates style analysis and text comparison can open student collaboration to insights into the effects of style and revision, adding another substantive level to collaborative writing and responding. Using software that works on word-processing files to provide text analysis (RightWriter) and text comparison (CompareRite) frees students from the drudgery of marking and comparing drafts, while concentrating students' focus on texts and readers.

I have taught writing in DePaul University's microcomputer classrooms since 1984. The courses have ranged from remedial and developmental through our standard freshman composition program to 200- and 300-level technical and professional writing. I have used labs with a variety of configurations: computers arranged in an L; arranged in a U; arranged in rows facing each other; and arranged in parallel rows, all facing in the same direction, like student seating in a traditional classroom. My classes have used IBM-compatible computers and advanced word-processing software, initially SAMNA II and III and then WordPerfect 4.0, 4.1, and 5.0. For the first few years, we had stand-alone computers; more recently, we have moved to classroom networks with word-processing software on a file server. The networked computers, like stand-alone computers with hard disks, facilitate the easy use of Thesaurus and Spell Check functions.

None of our university labs is exclusively for the use of writing students or for the use of a single department. All DePaul students have access to a variety of labs in various buildings on all of our campuses, so as students choose to congregate and write at a particular lab outside class time, they seem to be deliberately opting for continuing community beyond the writing classroom.

The physical setting of a computer lab—regardless of configuration, software, or hardware—has changed dynamics within the classroom. Rather than a hierarchical teacher–passive whole group, the lab situation naturally fragments or parcels the class into partnerships and small groups—arrangements often of necessity when students have to share a limited number of computers. As the lab decentralized the classroom, my role as instructor has changed. I am less of a judge and more of a consultant, guide, mentor, and adviser. My single authority is supplemented by the assistance and authority of peers, as groups work with the software and their projects. Grouping students is quite literally a necessity that is the mother of invention. Students form working partnerships and groups that move naturally from assisting each other with software to assisting each other with writing. What we have discovered is that the computer classroom and collaborative learning techniques enhance each other in a number of ways. The natural strengths of each tend to counteract problems with either alone.

Many group techniques in the traditional classroom can require structures unnatural to conversation and to putting peer suggestions into direct practice in inventing or revising writing. Most standard, noncomputer techniques for recording collaboration require extra work from students or extraneous technology. For example, Thom Hawkins (1976) asserts the need for a group secretary to take notes for group reports and the instructor's record of the group's progress, but Hawkins himself reports a student's questioning, "What incentive is there for anyone to take one of these positions?" (p. 18) Diana George (1984) reports a method of taping group sessions, responding to the tapes, and discussing group tapes with the whole class. Others have used videotape to record group discussion and suggestions.

The computer keyboard and disk storage seem to me a far more natural means of capturing peer collaboration and connecting to the writing process—a way for students to record their interactions, as well as a way to make those interactions and record an integral part of their inventing, drafting, and revising process. In the computer classroom, students' talking about writing and group writing becomes linked to keyboarding—trying peer suggestions and responding to alternatives immediately, using word-processing functions to invent, rearrange, and reinvent without disturbing the original text file. Students see interacting at and with the keyboard as more a privilege than a burden.

Before I used the computer classroom, some students reacted negatively to collaboration and especially to peer critiquing, feeling that they got little from sharing papers with their peers, that their papers were "cut up" by others, or that the time they had put into a project was wasted if reader responses indicated that the writer should "start over." Such complaints were essentially eliminated in computer lab collaboration. Students' emphasis went from critiquing as judging and criticizing to critiquing as suggesting, starting, and creating new plans and parts in the same session. The fluidity of computer text files and the immediate connection between peer response and collaboratively creating alternatives establishes a sense of continuous interaction between readers and writer.

In the computer classroom, collaboration begins with invention. Using a variety of invention techniques adapted to the collaborative environment of the computer classroom allows students to become foils and partners for each other in the act of invention—as well as available readers and critics of drafts, suggesters of alternatives, and pathfinders of techniques to find technological aids in editing and correction. The physical acts of sitting and working and writing together, both in and out of class, encourage students to see themselves as colleagues in the process of finding and forming ideas.

Collaborative invention techniques that introduce advanced word-processing functions—Blocking, Copying, and Moving text,

Switching between Documents, Moving text from one document or file to another—allow students to aid each other in becoming familiar and adept with functions that encourage a recursive writing process, movement between stages of the composing process and macro-level revisions.

An assortment of invention techniques combine the visual sharing (and neatness) of text on the computer monitor with word processing's ability to allow Adds, Deletions, Changes, and Moves while retaining "clean" copies of earlier versions. The ability to create a clear overall visual structure and the capacity to make print and disk copies for every member of the group (as well as the instructor) provide optimum conditions for group invention, while encouraging practice and group help in mastering word-processing functions that encourage flexible creation and revision.

INVENTION TECHNIQUES FOR THE COMPUTER CLASSROOM

List making	Partners and small groups make lists of potential paper topics for an assignment. Individuals may identify their contributions by using text-formatting functions like Underline and Bold.
Branching	Students branch topics into lists of specifics. Using the Insert function, Tabs, Returns, and (occasionally) Windows or Columns, students record ideas for specific development either under or to the right of their listed paper topics.
	As they discuss their lists, students use the Cursor keys and Insert function to move back and forth between specificity and the more general topic level. At this stage, students also frequently insert Returns to create blank space on the screen.
	As groups select items from their lists to develop further, they use the Block and Move functions to copy text from one part of the screen to another or to a different file or window. Frequently students move words or phrases from the specific

branch side of the screen over to the topics side to consider whether the specifics can themselves be paper topics. Students seem to find the ease of moving between categories—and moving between parts of the screen—increases their confidence in generating multiple options and in limiting topics.

Quasi-clusters

Small groups work to randomly fill the screen with words, either as a first invention activity or at any other stage. The writer uses Tabs and Returns to space material (though some students use Windows or Line Drawing) and uses Cursor Keys and Insert to place new words in the same locus. Students often revert to quasi-clusters after they have a limited topic, situation, and audience in mind.

Groups usually move their most likely clusters to a new screen and develop them with Branching or using basic questioning patterns: Who? What? When? Where? Why? How?

Marking clusters, lists, etc.

Partners use Block with Bold or Block with Underline to select ideas from the invention exercises. Using Block and Copy Block, individual writers move their choices to new working space without disturbing the group's original cluster or list.

Students often find most intriguing what has been marked by more than one partner (e.g., what is both Bolded and Underlined).

Fill in the blanks

Students working through ideas use the screen to display sentence patterns that spur invention. The simplest and most general pattern is _____ makes me think of _____, but we also generate more specific sentences tied to the subject area of a particular assignment.

After choosing a sentence pattern, the writer uses the Block and Copy Block functions to fill the monitor screen with the sentence pattern. Individual students can fill both blanks in a sentence, or partners/groups work together, with one student filling in the first blank and others filling in the second. Students sometimes Block and Copy Block to move words from the sentence patterns to other invention files. Some groups use fill-in-the-blanks sentences to further process words or phrases from list making or synonyms.

Chaining fill in the blanks

Students who like fill-in-the-blanks invention usually move to linking the sentences in the basic pattern (e.g., __A__ makes me think of __B__. __B__ makes me think of __C__.).

Groups usually quickly abandon such simple patterns and use Typeover or Insert to create more precise relationships between the chained words or phrases (e.g., changing __A__ makes me think of __B__. __A__ fits in category __B__.).

Groups usually ask questions like What kind of relationship is this? What kind of paper would this be? as they change their original pattern. Students also look for patterns within their filled-in blanks, often finding relationships within the left and right columns. Writers move words from the blanks when patterns seem to suggest a possible line of development for a paper.

Synonyms to there's more than one way

One writer generates synonyms for a topic or specific support, often using the Thesaurus function to supplement an initial list. A partner or small group comments on whether the new words seem synonymous in terms of the topic so far or whether they raise different connotations.

Groups usually work together to branch from each synonym to possible paper developments suggested by the word. Disagreements about what is synonymous often turn into discussions of how the topic might appear or appeal to different audiences.

Groups often proceed from their synonyms list to asking Who? When? Where? sorts of questions about audiences.

Planning

With general topics and supporting or connected ideas arranged on the monitor screen, groups use Windows or simple space creators like Tab to organize a list of thesis possibilities on another part of the screen.

Students use Block and Copy Block to move the likeliest theses to clean space in order to work out planning for audience and specific support—often reusing invention techniques. Although planning is usually scheduled in a separate class meeting, student groups often move back and forth between invention and specific paper planning.

Freewriting/ drafting

Writers move freely into freewriting or drafting text at any time, often by splitting the screen or by using the Switch function to display a new screen—Document 2—without needing to exit from Document 1. Writers often move freewriting text from the invention files and use it in some way in the paper. Students also Scroll through such "draft" text either marking (as with Underline) or Copying Blocks of text into paper plans.

Collaboration and the freedom implicit in the invention techniques carry through in individual writers' drafting. In class sessions devoted to drafting, students in pauses consulted their partners or went back to reread their text, then added by inserting within the text rather than at the end of what they had previously written. (This kind of sequence is fairly easy to capture when students are instructed to Save at regular intervals in order to protect against accidental losses. Almost all students Save at the beginning of a pause and Save again when they have made a change.) Students also inserted multiple returns to give themselves clean space to write, some trying out radical changes of direction and mode and then deciding in a later session whether to go with an overall change or to incorporate some of the new material into the prior text. Sometimes the new material went out entirely, back into a prewriting file. Frequently text that appeared as a conclusion in an early draft became part of the introduction in later drafts.

As drafts develop, the class moves to reading and responding to work in progress. Initially, we use a quasi-Rogerian technique of retelling our readings. Conveying the reader respondent's sense of the text, these initial readings use prompts ("What I see is . . ." "What I hear is . . .") to report simple sense impressions. Retelling as a collaborative technique, using partner/group responses phrased as sense impressions, is especially useful in providing writers with a sense of what they have controlled or limited and what they have left uncontrolled or unstated.

On protocols or self-evaluations, students frequently comment on how partners' retelling affected the writers' sense of what they wanted their papers to do. Explaining their own revisions of language, order, or mode, students are remarkably assertive and responsive. Some sample comments:

> "They [paragraphs in original order] weren't getting across what I wanted."
>
> "I want this to say what I mean. I don't want to leave it open for anyone else to decide what I mean."
>
> "I know now that I find out what I want to say when I write. A draft is a way of finding that out. Now I know I need to change that sometimes to make sure that my readers find out what I found out."
>
> "I decide what my reader should hear."
>
> "I felt I could choose what was a keeper. I knew what they were seeing and what I hadn't shown them enough of."

For later critiquing and revising sessions, I encourage partners to comment on at least paragraph-length sections of text rather than inserting comments or corrections on specific words and sentences. I also encourage and ask groups to practice asking questions of the writer rather than making statements about the effectiveness or correctness of the writing. I have three reasons for this approach.

One, my research on relationships between editors and professional writers has shown that the most productive and least rancorous interactions are those in which the editor responds as a reader, dealing with textual problems by posing questions (Cyganowski 1988).

Two, much of the research on the effects of word processing on individual student writers reports that students using computers have tended toward surface, or micro-level revisions, editing rather than the substantive rethinking and changing we would generally consider revising. Combining word processing with collaboration and community building, while teaching functions that encourage substantive revision, seems a likely means of redirecting writers' attention to larger, composing issues. Having pairs of groups of students work together with a monitor and keyboard seems to distract collaborators from the individual writer's or reader's tendency to focus on surface editing—redirecting attention to issues of content, organization, sequence, development, support, and authority.

Three, many peer critiquing formats in the traditional classroom have focused on sentences (e.g., is the thesis clear?). In years past, I have observed my own students ignoring more general peer advice in favor of making specifically identified sentence-level corrections. Essentially, they were selecting only the micro-level when they used their peer responses as an agent in revising/editing their papers.

The following collaborative revision techniques and others students develop to suit their papers and relationship are based on a few common principles. Student partners generally respond to paragraphs, sections, partial drafts, or whole papers rather than to individual sentences, phrases, or words. Avoiding sentence-level comment at the revision stage tends to focus both writer's and readers' attention on substantive revision rather than surface-level changes or corrections. Partners are encouraged to respond with questions rather than statements. The writer and group attempt to answer the questions by posing alternatives.

COLLABORATIVE REVISION TECHNIQUES FOR THE COMPUTER CLASSROOM

Purpose partner(s) = audience	What are you asking me to understand? think? do? be? buy?
Generic questions	Who? What? When? Where? Why? How? Is this supposed to be good or bad? Do you think this is important? most important? Is this the only reason? Is this the best reason? Can you tell me how this connects?
Specific questions	Responses to specific content or topic, often variations on generic questions (e.g., Was it good or bad that Napoleon went ahead? Do you think bosses are the only reason someone loves or hates a job?).
Responses	Specific, sometimes argumentative: How'd he do that? [Request for causality] Not me. [Objection to overgeneralization] Apples and apples. [Objection to same level of specificity or to repetition] This could be anything. [Objection to vagueness, lack of concrete detail]
Personas as audience	Assuming personas, persons to be informed/persuaded/and so forth; identifying values and means: Say it was a biology teacher reading this. Say it was my Aunt Helen reading this.

Retelling   Often phrased in terms of sense impressions:
reading   What I hear is . . .
                  What I see is . . .
                  Do you mean . . . ?

Using disks to store successive versions of the same text in different files and having partners use Underline mode to highlight their comments allow me to see the effect of these techniques, to see which revising and editing decisions are likely responses to peer comment and collaboration. I am also able to see an overview of each student's progress within successive stages of a particular writing assignment and over the course of a quarter. With each new assignment, I reserve the possibility of reforming the groups so that students who are strong in dealing with certain kinds of problems are matched with others who could most benefit.

What I see on disk is students' growing awareness and practice of writing as a process. In revising, they move material out of draft files and back into prewriting files. As different readers respond to their texts, writers realize that parts of their drafts were explorations, means to deciding what they wanted to say. I find frequent changes of introductions and conclusions as responses to partner reading and questioning.

In developing papers through collaborative reading and revision, partners aid the writer's answering questions and forming alternatives. A group may generate as many as five solutions to a problem, ranging from rewording or adding to a single sentence through rearranging or reshaping the whole paper or a major section.

Reviewing the revisions from a year's worth of freshman composition classes (more than 100 students, more than 400 papers) showed papers from the collaborative computer classroom undergoing substantial change in the revision process. More than 50 percent of the student papers showed changes in introductions and changes in the order of paragraphs, as well as additions of detail to individual paragraphs and increased specificity or more precise diction.

Nearly 20 percent of the papers showed wholesale changes in organization or approach—new drafts from some point after the introduction or changes in the overall approach or mode (e.g., restarting in a different mode, as in moving from narrative to comparison, or using pieces of an earlier draft in a new form and order). Such large-scale changes usually corresponded to movement of material between invention, drafting, and revision files, indicating students' decisions that parts or all of a draft were prewriting or students' returns to invention files to retrieve material to start again. Students seem quite aware of what they are doing when they move text between invention and draft files, sometimes even commenting with notes to me in their files (e.g., "Dear Dr. C: I only learned what I had to say as I wrote it. This isn't really a draft. The draft's in the next file now."). More than 20 percent of the papers also showed writers adding alternative explanations and attempting to sort through alternatives, adding complexity to earlier generalizations or assertions.

A smaller number of papers showed interest in and revisions of figurative language. Nearly 10 percent of the papers revealed deletions of trite images or comparisons and deletions of consciously created images. Other file/draft sequences showed writers working to make deliberate choices of whether to delete, retain, or change figurative language—often trying to rework and keep a phrase when readers misunderstood it on first reading.

What has intrigued me is that the students don't describe such changes as revising. What I would call revision—material changes and reworking—they classified as "still writing." Rather than having a step-by-step view of invention, draft, revision, they were increasingly recursive. They moved from draft back to invention techniques to reclassifying parts of the draft as invention or freewriting. They felt free to move text from place to place and file to file, some copying text to as many as eight different places in a paper and leaving this copied text in place through a couple of successive revisions. When I commented on such techniques, students were surprised I hadn't tried them myself. One man pointed out that it was a way to really use his partners. "Since they don't always get to read the whole thing, I wait to see where it strikes them as out of place and to see when I have prepared for it. I think that part is what's going to be close to the final version of the thesis. I don't like it at the beginning or end. I want to build on it, so I'm keeping it around. Besides, it reminds me."

Students in the collaborative computer classes also frequently remind each other, in and out of class, of what needs to be built into a paper. After turning in a draft to me, collaborative students frequently go ahead with revisions, using their partners' and their own responses as guides. They seem confident that they have a sense of what's weak and how to fix it, without waiting for me to read and return the draft—even though I usually return them at the next class session two days later. In self-evaluations of papers, students articulate their own and their partners' awareness of problems in a draft: "Many times I needed to elaborate or give more detail on things I made reference to in order to make things more clear." "I couldn't decide exactly what position to take in writing the paper so I really didn't take one. Instead, I shifted from one idea to another without really making any connections between them."

In peer and self-evaluations, students frequently remind themselves of former behavioral or attitudinal impediments to writing—habits that kept them from becoming engaged with their writing. One woman's revelatory testimonial highlights how the immediacy of collaboration pushes reluctant students into becoming writers in a community.

> I procrastinate when a first idea doesn't work out. Even though I know I can always get my partners to try alternatives. So this quarter, I felt I couldn't let them down by not trying again myself, and the class made me try again right away, because the others were waiting on me. Now, with other courses, instead of putting something aside and procrastinating when I can't get it right the first time, I catch myself talking to myself, asking questions to me about what else I can try. People must think I'm crazy, but now I talk to myself and then start again or start in a different place and keep on going until I have something, even if I know it's not great.

Such comments and personal responsibility mark major changes from what I observed before collaboration and computers. My students had tended to see me, not themselves, as the party responsible for identifying any problems and the specific "corrections" that would move a paper to perfection—or at least to a grade of A. The kind of comment I used to get focused on grading. The typical student's lament, "I felt as though in my revision I corrected everything commented on in my rough draft and therefore expected a higher grade than I received," was very different from the self-evaluations now that comment, however generally, on the writing itself. Students now congratulate themselves on accomplishments in revisions (comments that seldom mention either grades or me as judge): "I actually learned something about what I was talking about and tried to say something instead of talking a lot about nothing." "Saying only things that really matter. NO B.S.ing—this may result in a short paper—but no B.S."

Editing final or near-final text is a stage when many students wish to revert to a single, outside authority. To foster continuing collaboration and more thoughtful consideration of standards of correctness and style, I encourage students to take control of their own editing decisions by engaging them in "playing" with the word-processing software. Inventing ways to use the program to flag writing problems, students have necessarily become more conscious of their own editing needs. Search is the most frequently used function in students' efforts toward systematic editing, for example,

> Search for "you" or "you*" to flag shifts in person.
> Search for "they" or "their" to flag possible shifts in number.
> Search for "is," "are," and so forth to identify passives.
> Search for "*ed" and "have" to flag potential problems with verb usage.
> Search for "to *" and "of *" to identify possible strings of prepositional phrases.
> Search for "no" and "not" to identify negatives.
> Search for particular problem phrases, e.g.,
> "due to the fact that"
> "at this point in time"
> "reason is * because"
> "is when"
> "is where."
> Search for "it's" (and its').

The Count feature of Search also intrigues students, some of whom track the decreasing occurrence of their particular problem phrases and celebrate when a bothersome quirk disappears from their draft (e.g., "I don't due-to-the-fact-that any more.").

"Playing" with the word-processing program and group editing turns up a plethora of uses for different functions. For example, WordPerfect's Spell Checker Look Up function, which searches the dictionary for words or word patterns, has proven a delightful way to find rhymes or alliterative words. Students create Look Up patterns with a few letters and the wild card *, generating lists of words that rhyme or alliterate. One hundred-level students seem to increase their sense of what letter patterns produce the same sounds by collaboratively composing searches, starting by looking for rhymes using the letter combinations in their original word (e.g., sign was first entered as a Look Up: *ign). Another group member suggested trying *ine. Another, intrigued by how many vowels would produce the sound, tried *yne. Such playfulness occasionally produces striking rhyming combinations. (My favorite so far is see/sea/anemone.) More importantly, students who are unaccustomed to thinking of the way words sound or of dictionaries as creative, useful tools involve themselves and others in seeking out varieties of language they've never considered before. ESL students are especially taken with discovering what different letter combinations can produce the same sound and that the same letter combinations produce different sounds. Professional writing students, especially those with a bent toward writing advertising copy and catchy headlines, often spend a half-hour brainstorming together on combinations to Look Up for rhymes or alliterations.

Editing sessions also lead to full-class discussions of diction, audience, and authorial authority—especially when some writers have used the Thesaurus with a heavy hand. Students often come out of a peer editing session wanting more general discussion of issues that have arisen from considering their own and their partners' papers. They pose issues to the class (sometimes, it seems, as an alternative to direct conflict with a partner). For example, one student opened a discussion of diction by saying, "So many people try to sound impressive by using large words that sound great, [except] they don't really know what these words mean."

Although specialized applications programs designed to deliver instruction have been decried as often as praised, commercially available professional software can be used in class and by students to enhance collaboration, as it automates and aids production of data on which collaboration can be based. Especially to spur deliberate discussion of usage and style standards, I have found that add-on text analysis and style checkers (e.g., RightWriter and Grammatik) free student writers and collaborators from both mechanical proofreading and personal conflict. Text analysis software like RightWriter produces an annotated version of a file, marking features like long sentences, passives, weak diction, and potentially offensive language. With RightWriter's marking the text according to a professional standard of clear and effective writing, student partners can focus on discussing and revising—making deliberate choices as to whether the "standard" should be applied in a given situation for a given audience. Working with RightWriter's analysis of their texts, collaborators discuss the effects of stylistic options, focusing on the appropriateness of diction and syntax choices in the specific paper.

As word processing takes away the drudgery of retyping, moving, reformatting, and copying text—and allows students to retain original copy as well as copy commented on by peers and instructor—text analysis and text comparison software can take away the drudgery of analyzing style and comparing revisions. Such software allows and encourages students to focus on macro, holistic questions of purpose, rhetorical strategy, effect, and audience.

Commercial software designed for group writing projects and document management can truly come of age in the collaborative composition classroom. Working with word-processing files, students can use software like CompareRite (originally designed by JURISOFT for legal applications) to very quickly compare and mark changes in two versions of the same document or paper. CompareRite performs the mechanics of comparison, identifying and marking insertions, deletions, and moves—with the users choosing the format in which changes are marked, including choices between comparisons of passages as large blocks and comparisons that display variants word by word. Students can use

CompareRite to consider their own revision processes. Collaborators who have responded to various drafts of a paper can use text comparison to identify exactly what textual variants have caused them to respond differently to separate versions of the same paper.

In the process of peer reading, commenting, and revising, students have reacted to their partners' drafts, responding mostly with questions addressed to whole passages or whole works rather than to individual lines or words. Collaborators have looked for what provoked a question and have formed alternatives for revision. As partners review new drafts, they often read both the earlier draft and the revision, asking themselves questions like How is the overall effect different? What made the difference?

After some weeks of using collaborative invention and revision techniques, partners can use CompareRite to look at revisions and their effects. Text-comparison software readily supplies the data necessary to answer students' questions about differences by marking the variations between draft files. Working with CompareRite displays and printouts, partners examine the highlighted changes in collated text in order to jointly analyze how specific changes led to differences in effect and effectiveness noted by readers. Students also seem to find particularly interesting the number and kind of textual changes that readers have not noticed.

We try to follow any text comparison session with short, journal-like papers, summarizing or just listing what changes or revisions appear to lead to different reader perceptions of the revised text. (Students are also asked to reflect on their own writing processes, to consider how directly a revision resulted from collaboration, and to try to recall which revisions were tied to other revisions in the same text.) Using text-comparison software to study one's own revision processes and to see the effects of revision in other writers' work has enhanced students' valuing of both the collaboration and the revision processes.

As the course continues and these insights are shared, groups and, finally, the class as a whole try to form generalizations about how certain kinds of revisions affect readers' responses to texts. Depending on the nature of the assignments and the level of the class, our generalizations have noted that draft conclusions moved into introductions seem to clarify the overall direction of a paper and to enhance reader understanding; that appeals to authority that follow a writer's presentation of other evidence seem more persuasive to readers than appeals to authority that come before the writer's own evidence; and that the addition of transitional passages can be either effective or irritating, depending on whether or not readers see the transitions as fully integrated into the paper's development. Students writing arguments have discovered through text comparison that the process of collaborative reading and revision has led them to some fairly regular patterns of revision: reordering arguments, more expressly warranting their claims, adding paragraphs of backing for their warrants, and deleting repetitions and personal asides.

Over the past five years, DePaul students have responded positively to increasing use of word-processing and other software and to the collaborative computer classroom. In course-end evaluations from the collaborative computer classes, more than 90 percent of the students report that using computers in groups changed their attitudes toward writing and helped improve their writing. In the free-response sections of evaluations, students consistently comment that they plan to continue using the computer lab, not only to use word processing but also to work where other writers are working, to find readers, or to develop collaborative projects.

Since none of our university labs is assigned to writing students or designated for the use of a single department, all DePaul students have access to a variety of labs in various buildings on all of our campuses. Students who choose to continue to congregate and write at a particular lab thus seem deliberately to be choosing an option for continuing a kind of community outside and beyond their writing classes. The power of collaboration in combining community with technology is evidenced as well by regular complaints from students in classes where I don't use the computer classroom for group work. They truly seem to see the absence of collaborative computer assignments as a loss of fellowship and audience and of a natural gathering place for students outside class. Availability of computer labs and freedom to use them for class projects are "not the same" without the practice of collaboration.

In the 1988–1989 academic year, DePaul University began a pilot program of building word processing into all 100-level writing courses. A hands-on introduction to word processing was a component of all course sections, but the amount and nature of word-processing instruction varied, with formats ranging from support staff teaching word-processing functions in a single class meeting through fully collaborative curricula.

The first group of sections had one class session of training—an introduction to the lab, computer system, and basic WordPerfect functions (including Block and Move)—taught by academic support staff. A few of these sections were offered the same introduction on videotape.

The second group of sections had training in two class sessions, a week apart—an introduction to the lab, computer system, and WordPerfect functions in a sequence designed by writing faculty to simulate the order in which functions were most likely to be used in the writing process. These sections were taught by staff from our Academic Computer Services department.

The third group of sections had introductions to WordPerfect taught by the classroom instructors and integrated with class assignments. These sections also met in the computer lab for one to three additional sessions using WordPerfect for inventing, drafting, or revising.

The fourth group of sections learned WordPerfect from each other and the instructor, while working on class assignments in collaborative groups. These collaborative sections met in the computer lab for at least one class session per week, and almost all these students created most stages of each assignment in the lab, in or out of class.

Student evaluations of the pilot program revealed tangible differences in responses to the collaborative sections—reactions that suggest the value of combining computers with collaboration in the writing classroom. Although the majority of all students in all instruction formats found word-processing instruction very useful or somewhat useful, the students taught by staff (rather than by their own instructors) were less likely to use word processing outside of class and less likely to find that it had improved their writing. Students taught by their own instructors and scheduled for more class sessions in the lab used word processing more outside of class, and they were also somewhat more likely to find that it had improved their writing. However, students in the collaborative sections all found their word-processing instruction very useful; all used word processing and the university computer labs outside of class; and all found that it had improved their writing. In the "any additional comments" section of the evaluation, most of the collaborative students volunteered comments that they had switched to composing at the keyboard and that they felt collaboration combined with word processing had improved not only their writing skills but also their ability to read critically.

WORKS CITED

Cyganowski, Carol Klimick. *Magazine Editors and Professional Authors in Nineteenth-Century America: The Genteel Tradition and the American Dream.* New York: Garland, 1988.

George, Diana. "Working with Peer Groups in the Composition Classroom." *College Composition and Communication* (October 1984): 320–326.

Hawkins, Thom. *Group Inquiry Techniques for Teaching Writing.* Urbana, IL: ERIC Clearinghouse on Reading and Communication Skills, National Institute of Education, 1976.

Computers and the Social Contexts of Writing

KATHLEEN SKUBIKOWSKI
Middlebury College
JOHN ELDER
Middlebury College

When we incorporated computers into our composition courses five years ago, we wanted to explore the ways in which word processing changed both the thinking and writing processes of our students and our own writing pedagogy[1] in our freshman writing classes. We had always employed group brainstorming, exploratory writing, peer editing, and multiple revisions. By designing collaborative environments within the classroom, we had hoped to encourage our students to approach reading and writing with an understanding of their social contexts, in part because the process approach can isolate novice writers, each intent upon his or her own sequence of drafts. We had always felt most comfortable with what James Moffett calls the "process of *expatiation* that takes the interplay of inner voices back out into the social world where the give and take of minds and voices can take each member of the community beyond where he or she started" (1982, p. 234). We didn't want, by introducing computers, to lose sight of our central values as teachers of writing, or of the good things that were already happening in our classes. We didn't want computers to replace on a primitive level the fairly sophisticated human interactions our students were already achieving. Instead, our aim was to help our students develop a viable role for the computer in their intellectual lives, in their lives as maturing writers in a writing community.

In questioning colleagues about the impact of computers on their students' writing and on their own writing pedagogy, we had received certain warnings. The computer indeed facilitates the production and revision of text, we heard, but the ease of word processing tempts novice writers to verboseness and blurs for them crucial distinctions between proofreading and revising. Students are tempted, as well, toward premature closure. Deceived by polished output, they come to equate good formatting with good text. (How could anything with justified right margins be poorly written?) Encouraging students to compose and revise on the screen can also introduce unnecessary anxiety and inhibitions. Terminals may simply not be available when inspiration strikes; computer rooms are often alienating and inhibiting; the small chunks of text visible at one time make global revision seem impossible and encourage tinkering at the word-and-sentence levels.

A coherent pedagogy for computer writing has been slow in emerging. In "The User-Friendly Fallacy" (1987), Fred Kemp articulates some of the problems. Computer-supported writing instruction remains dominated by grammar drill, text analysis, and unsophisticated word processing. If properly developed and applied, he argues, computer technology can do much more than simply cosmeticize text or drill students on the avoidance of comma splices. Such uses have remained undeveloped, according to Kemp, because of the "user-friendly fallacy"—the belief that for a computer to provide truly significant help to the student writer it must (a) produce the illusion of actual person-to-person interaction and (b) evaluate the content and quality of student input.

In developing our courses we chose to avoid all programs for drill and practice, parsing, or brainstorming programs—then illusions of human interaction or of human evaluation. We had long believed, with Kenneth Bruffee, that "the first steps to learning to think better . . . are learning to converse better and learning to establish and maintain the sorts of social context, the sorts of community life, that foster the sorts of conversation members of the community value" (1984, p. 640). Therefore, we decided to explore how word processing might help us establish a community of writers and might facilitate that interplay of voices in an educational context. Our decision was to combine word processing and networking within a system that encouraged our students to work together in developing their ideas and shaping their language. We wanted to emphasize the fluidity and the ephemeral qualities of writing done on a computer, to draw on the technology for both its speed and its potential for playfulness.

That much decided, we organized a pilot course called "Journal and Essay." Each of our sections of 15 students met in a large classroom equipped with 18 Macintosh Pluses, three printers, and one Macintosh SE dedicated as a file server using Appleshare. The microcomputers were networked, allowing students to print from any terminal in the room and allowing access to the file server either from the Macs in the room or via modem from computers in dorm rooms and faculty offices. The Macintosh Pluses were placed at stations around the walls, and there was a large seminar table in the middle of the classroom. Chairs on casters allowed students to face each other during class discussion, to move together for small-group work, or to work at the computers. We devoted the first week of class to introducing the basic skills of word processing using Microsoft Word. By the beginning of the second week, students could handle disks, write text onto them, copy files, format basic essays, and print.

During that second week we began the system of daily exploratory writing that would become the basis for all other work on reading and writing in the course. We explained to our students that they would be responsible every week for writing five exploratory entries of about 30 minutes each onto their disks. Their entries are modeled on freewrites of the Elbow/Macrorie sort, though they were formed into a somewhat more focused and continuous sequence. Students would plunge into explorations that might arise from readings (we read William Zinsser's *On Writing Well* [1985], Donald Hall's *The Contemporary Essay* [1984], and William Smart's *Eight Modern Essayists* [1985]), issues raised in class discussion, or events in their lives.

Not all of the daily entries developed further; in fact, most did not. But some did serve as the seeds from which more extended, formal essays for the course grew. Periodically, students would combine some of the writings they had done into a longer piece with a central focus, by concatenating files and cutting and pasting paragraphs to see what different orders the ideas might go in, what different shapes the ideas might take—all with the ease that only a computer can offer. At midterm and again at the semester's end, each student would submit a portfolio of three completed essays for a grade. As students experimented with this organic method of writing formal essays, they began noticing that writing became easier, that they had more to say, that their voices sounded less stiff, and that the speed of the computer was, as one of them put it, "bringing writing and thinking closer together."

By the third week of the course, we introduced our system of networked "corresponding" by which the usefulness of the computer could be taken beyond word processing.[2] After the students wrote for five days, they deposited their week's entries from disks onto the Appleshare network. Then each student would call up the week's writing of two assigned classmates, read it through, and respond to it both with interlinear comments and by writing a letter at the end of the file. The correspondents were not evaluating the entries on the level of correctness, but indicating instead which elements were engaging and why, and where they as audience would encourage the writer to delve more deeply. None of this writing was graded by us; we simply browsed, occasionally corresponded, and recorded the entries and responses as completed on time or not. Timely corresponding accounted for one-fifth of the total grade.

The advantages of combining word processing with collaboration on the network became apparent to us almost immediately, although perhaps not so quickly to our students. Even though we had purposely kept the technology at a minimal level of complexity, our students' initial reactions to the class ranged from curiosity to misunderstanding and fear. As one of the more intimidated students admitted at midterm,

> I remember being very frightened on the first day of class [thinking] that our sole means of communication would be on the computer. I figured that I would never get the hang of using a computer, and from the very beginning had reason to believe that my supposition was true. For the first two weeks of class, I daily encountered some problem. . . . But by the fourth week, [I] began to look forward to the time spent on the computer . . . and was amazed at how fast it made the whole process.

As the course progressed, the quality of the final drafts in their portfolios indicated that our students were indeed accumulating an impressive repertoire of writing strategies, many of them learned from each other on the network. The portfolios indicated, too, that our novice writers were clearly aware of their audiences and of the ways in which interaction from the very earliest stages of a piece could help them identify, connect, and deepen promising material. One student's correspondents pointed out to her that in 7 of her first 15 daily entries, regardless of the initial topic, her thoughts turned at some point to the U.S. Ski Team and her disappointment at not having made it. In a subsequent entry she discussed rereading those entries and then shaping them into a formal essay.

> All of my formal pieces have stemmed from my weekly entries. The one that really popped unexpectedly out was the one relating to the U.S. Ski Team. I did not intentionally mean to focus on skiing in any of my entries, it just turned out that way. No matter what subject I started off with, skiing would always enter into the story line one way or another. It was a very good thing to have me verbalize my feelings toward the team, and incorporate my own experiences into the bigger picture in a paper [a researched essay on the ski industry]. I obviously have many strong feelings concerning skiing, and it was quite a chore to find a solid direction in my final copy, but I think it was a worthwhile struggle. I learned a lot about myself and my attitude in that particular writing.

It was our sense that the system had several advantages for our students beyond the quality of their portfolio essays, and that these advantages found their fullest expression in the experience of participating in a community of writers. The energy, commitment, and collaboration generated on the network penetrated every aspect of the course. Both inside and outside the classroom, students gained a personal agenda as writers and a context within which their individual work, for our class and for others, could be carried out. One student compared the atmosphere of corresponding in our class with peer critiquing in her studio art classes.

> The emphasis in learning has broken the traditional "student only learns from the teacher" method. One reason this kind of teaching method is so valuable to me is that it creates a kind of bond among

students; we are all in this together, and here to learn. In discussing or critiquing our work with other students, it sets up a kind of support system which I find important to the learning process.

Another student indicated that, as we had hoped, the discussions were being carried on outside the classroom as well.

> Even when not in class, I find that fellow classmates, from different sections even, share ideas, inspirations, frustrations. In this way, my trip to the computer room for an hour every day often turns into much longer and becomes a place of interaction between myself and fellow writers. I've really noticed a great change in my writing. It still has a long way to go, but it has also come a long way in the last few weeks. I've also applied what I've learned from this class to other situations and writing environments. This is, in my opinion, the real purpose of a course. It should have an impact on you long after the course is completed.

Other class members noted the value of "getting to know the people in class through their entries" and of "an unspoken trust" established between writer and correspondent, one that carried over into classroom discussions as well.

> I think that in this class, not only are we learning to write better, but we are also learning how to communicate. Well, that was rather a broad statement. What I mean is that within the fifteen or so people in our class, we are able to have unbiased conversations through the computer because one person writes all of his ideas (without interruption) and then the responding person gets a complete picture and may respond. This is a neat way to practice conversation. As for our in-class conversations, we have been able to get to know each other's writing, to know where each wants to go, and we are able to feel free to say what we think. Getting to know people on an intellectual basis and at the same time an extremely personal basis (for example, people write some of their deepest thoughts and emotions down) is one of the great features of this class.

Students' experience of participating in a social and, at the same time, intellectual activity was enhanced by the fluid and ephemeral nature of writing done on a computer. Boundaries between various forms of discourse blurred. The computer also helped their writing in ways they had not anticipated, as the daily exploratory writing provided them with an ideal forum for "getting things out," a process they often described as therapeutic.

I really enjoy working on it. I haven't been getting the mental blocks that I used to when faced with a blank piece of paper. Writing doesn't seem so painful when I know that my words are just so many dots of light on a screen.

I really like "playing computer" as my roommate has come to call it because of the fun I have when I come down to the computer room to just let my thoughts flow. The computer room has become quite a social place which adds a nice atmosphere to the whole game as well.

I actually like the feeling in the computer room of all the minds churning out so many different ideas and thoughts. As if thoughts were visible . . .

It's amazing the change that has come over me in my attitude towards computers. I don't find it difficult at all to express myself on them. . . . in fact, it can be a lot easier in some ways because you don't really have to worry about the permanence of what you are writing.

This issue of "permanence" in the last student's entry, echoed in various forms by his classmates, speaks to another of our main emphases in the course design: writing to learn. As the students corresponded and we browsed, we heard them talk of discovering that their personal thoughts, experiences, and reactions were shared by their classmates. Theirs were not necessarily unique and idiosyncratic ideas, as they had expected, but once articulated, were capable of being reflected on, illuminated. Like writing, they discovered, learning is a constant process of discarding, connecting, and reorganizing. We, in turn, were reminded by their comments of the shift Peter Elbow (1985) described from the indelibility of written language back toward the seemingly ephemeral nature of speech. Discussing freewriting, Elbow wrote,

> The potentiality in writing that I want to highlight here does not just involve generative techniques for getting first drafts written quicker, but rather a genuine change in mentality or consciousness. The original development of writing long ago permitted a new mentality that fostered thinking that was more careful, detached, and logical. But along with it and the indelibility that makes writing valuable came also a mentality that tends to lock us into our views once we

have carefully worked them out in writing. In contrast, the cultivation of writing as ephemeral fosters the opposite mentality whereby we use discourse (and writing in particular) not so much to express what we think, but rather to develop and transform it. (p. 289)

Although Elbow's context differs from ours, and his "discourse" emphasizes internalized and individualized dialogue, this more fluid sense of written language may be the most important feature of a pedagogy for computer writing.[3] It was precisely that ability to develop and transform their material that delighted us in our students' work. Through corresponding with the computer they came to understand revision as reseeing and deepening their original visions—often with the help of someone else's eyes. They discovered that their own texts were open, capable of being entered anywhere, by anyone, at the click of a mouse. As they continued expanding the possibilities for collaborating on their network, we found ourselves reading multiple versions of pieces in progress, versions students rarely called "drafts." More often they would say that, inspired by a correspondent's comment, they had been "playing" with a piece again. Similarly, we found correspondents returning to entries they had read in previous weeks to see how the pieces were evolving, sometimes regularly reading the work of certain classmates whose styles they liked or whose interests they found compatible with their own.

Throughout the semester we remained purposely vague on the subject of what type of corresponding might be most helpful, allowing them to develop their own criteria, which we periodically discussed in class. They quickly discarded as useless such general comments as "I like your entry" or "This is an interesting piece," and began to demand of each other more thoughtful and specific interactions. Their sense of mutual support within the network community did not lead to undiscriminating enthusiasm for each other's work. Rather, because students had a context for constructive criticism, their correspondence through Appleshare was quite pointed. We often found, for instance, that even before class they were already "discussing" their assigned readings on the network. One student wrote of her strong reaction to a piece by Maxine Hong Kingston, an excerpt in Hall (1984) called "No Name Woman" from *Woman Warrior*. In the piece, Kingston described the fate of her aunt in China: Cast out by her fellow villagers for becoming pregnant while her husband was off working in America, she drowned herself and her baby in the village well. The student's entry included the following passage:

> I can't believe how little pain I have had when I read something like "No Name Woman." I cried. I saw myself in that horrible small room, crouching in the corner, maybe under the bed, praying with everything I had that they would not find me, that somehow I could survive—that my baby would not really die. I found myself cursing the villagers. People are so goddamned heartless. They (I guess I should say "we" for I am human too) are so blind. We trap ourselves in superstitions and cling to them, turning away from a truer reality—like human need. Instead of helping each other to survive, we hunt each other down and kill each other. And, in our infinite wisdom we convince ourselves that what we are doing is the right thing to do. How did this happen, that we allow a mother to kill herself and let her baby die? How do we function from day to day knowing that there is a well that no longer runs clear?

Rather than simply praise the honesty and directness of the entry, this student's respondent began by writing,

> I was wondering if you could try to view the situation from the villagers' side. I know that it seems inhuman the way that they punish her, but if you look at their story, you may see some sort of reason behind their actions.

This correspondent went on to consider the sociology of a village during a time of famine, when most of the men were working abroad and sending their earnings back home. She was stimulated to a directness comparable to the original student's, and a dialogue was established through which the two of them approached the complexity and ambivalence of Kingston's original piece.

One student began an exploration by talking about a short essay by Eudora Welty called "The Little Store." It described a place of powerful associations from that author's childhood, and made him want to think about physical places with special importance in his growing up. He soon moved away from Welty's piece and launched into a description so vivid that one of his correspondents for the week singled it out. Here is the exploration itself, exactly as the writer spun it out in one quickly written entry on the computer.

I've just finished reading "The Little Store," and it has prompted me to think about such places in my world.

Let me tell you about the third floor of my house, or rather, the first and third floors.

The third floor is a wonderful maze of junk, fermenting in time. All the childhoods have been stored away in boxes to be saved, or sold at some yard sale in an unforeseen spring. Here the floors are rough, unpainted boards, with rugs of incalculable age stretching their fabric across their own worn spots. The ceiling is low, and the dust balls triumph in their haven. The ceiling has fallen and is plastered up with a little of the pink fiberglass still showing through. There are holes in one of the plaster board walls, and a bookshelf is littered with dusty and well read volumes bought second hand. Though this place seems old, it is really the center of all youthful activity in the house. The rooms of two older siblings are here as well as a small study and a lounge area with faded sofas bursting their seams. One room has no bedstead, but a futon covered with blankets and a warm, friendly cat. Though the ceiling is falling, some of the walls have been painted to look like an extra window, and the chimney bears the name of the patron saint (ghost) of this hide away, "RALF" in large graceful letters. The holes in the wall were made by adolescents' angers, and one now holds a red silk rose. The study is filled with diaries, one of my sibling's future memoirs. That's the philosopher. The books are old and tattered, yet are well absorbed classics of Kant, Descartes, Hemingway, Steinbeck, Wolfe, Mann . . . mostly thinker's books. These of course aren't far from the old Scribner's volumes of King Arthur, or Roland, or other such well read childhood tales. Every book has been conservatively pencilled in by the original reader, with signals to important passages, or an insightful thought about a certain quote. There is no phone or television, and the dusty windows are far above the traffic noises and give a high view on the hills outside. There's barely room to walk, yet intellectually, this is the highpoint in the household. This is where the youth, with their progressive ideas spend their time. This is where new music is listened to, or new experiences take place. For me, the most peacefully refreshing place I know is in this stuffy, cluttered attic.

At this point the writer moved to a description of the polished and sterile atmosphere of his home's living room.

The person who responded to this entry identified it as an energetic interesting piece of writing—well worth working up as an essay. She didn't bother pointing to problems with sentence structure, or paragraphing. Obviously, this exploration was written in a rush, with descriptive details pouring out under the pressure of powerful emotions. But this correspondent did discriminate in a general way between what she found the more impressive aspect of the entry and what was, possibly, expendable.

> Although all of your files are interesting, this is by far the best written and most effective as a reader-grabber. I mean, the description in the first paragraph about Floor #3 is fabulous. I like the movement in a supposedly (or typically) stagnant place, for example, the dust balls "triumphing." Also I noticed some great contrasts that you set up, such as the part about the junk being old, but the place is actually the center of "youthful activity," and the phrase that although there's barely room to walk, it's the "intellectual high point" of the house. Those "contrasts" (for lack of a better word) make the observations interesting and kind of move the piece along.
>
> I don't like the part about the first floor nearly as much, and not only because I'm sure that, like you, I wouldn't like the first floor as much. It's just not as well written, not as moving, not as clear of a picture in my mind. If you were to make a comparative essay, contrasting the first and third floors of the house, I would suggest that you bolster up the first floor part. (After all, the poor first floor can't beat the third in reality, so it wouldn't be fair to not even write effectively about it.) Notice how in the first floor description you practically always use the stupid-awful-boring verb TO BE. (the furniture IS, the rugs ARE, there IS, etc.) But if you weren't going to do both floors in one essay, the stuff you've got about the third floor alone would make a great descriptive kind of essay.

The original writer liked the suggestion for focusing on just the third floor, and came up with an essay that retained the vividness of that description while also developing a firmer sense of order and structure. He began the new essay with a description of the third floor, eliminating the slow lead of the original piece. He developed the idea of "childhoods" with details about outgrown clothes and discarded toys. He added visual details to his description of the attic's roof and floor and reorganized the material on his brother's and sister's rooms. These changes contributed to a more subtle and effective essay.

We felt both surprised and inspired by our students' work in the first year of the networked writing class. Each student had produced, we estimated, between 120 and 150 pages of writing, much of it of high quality. In one section, all the class members had, on their own, collaborated to produce a science fiction story.

At semester's end, they polished, formatted, and printed it, using a desktop publishing program. We now regularly introduce desktop publishing at the end of each semester, so that students can work together to publish a volume of their selected essays and exploratory entries. To encourage their playful collaboration, we also introduced an in-class writing game called "Musical Computers."[4] A 50-minute exercise which we use two or three times each semester, Musical Computers also takes particular advantage of the speed of computers and the fluid quality of text on a screen. We began by dividing the class into teams of four. Everyone would read a selected passage of literature, like this passage from the "Higher Laws" chapter of *Walden*:

> As I came home through the woods with my string of fish, trailing my pole, it being now quite dark, I caught a glimpse of a woodchuck stealing across my path, and felt a strange thrill of savage delight, and was strongly tempted to seize and devour him raw; not that I was hungry then, except for that wildness which he represented. Once or twice, however, while I lived at the pond, I found myself ranging the woods, like a half-starved hound, with a strange abandonment, seeking some kind of venison which I might devour, and no morsel could have been too savage for me. The wildest scenes had become unaccountably familiar. I found in myself, and still find, an instinct toward a higher, or, as it is named, spiritual life, as do most men, and another toward a primitive rank and savage one, and I reverence them both. I love the wild not less than the good.

Each student would begin by writing a one-paragraph assertion about the passage, and then everyone would get up and move down one terminal to the left. On the new screen, each student inherited someone else's opening paragraph. The idea now was to write a second paragraph employing a quotation from the original reading that would back up the previous student's assertion. Ten minutes later the writers would move to a third screen to add a complicating paragraph, something that contradicted the first two, gave the thinking a new twist, or went off on a pertinent digression. This, the students told us, was the difficult paragraph. Finally, 10 minutes later, at the fourth screen, each student would write a concluding paragraph that would draw the previous three together and synthesize the mini-dialectic that had just occurred, bringing in key phrases or images from the first and third paragraphs.

When the students returned to their original screens, they found that the pieces they had started had gone off in directions they had not anticipated, to conclusions they might not have drawn on their own. Their assignment for the next class was to survey the piece for obvious errors or awkwardness, run it through the spell-checker, and give it a title. At the beginning of the next class, as we read aloud a sampling of their pieces, the students discovered that writing produced by their collaborative efforts might be whimsical and quirky, but it was not pat or predictable writing. And, as in the following sample, it often showed energy:

> The most striking concept that Thoreau deals with in his passage is man's animalistic instincts and their place in a moral world. There can be no doubt of our origins. We began and evolved from a primal or animalistic state. Hence we all possessed at one time the survival or animal instinct Thoreau alludes to in his passage. The question is, now that we have "evolved" socially into a state where morality supposedly governs our actions, what has happened to our animalistic instincts? Thoreau doesn't try to mask or rationalize these instincts in man and himself, he revels in them. The wild is not to be less loved than the good, he declares. We do not have to be ashamed of such desires, they are a part of our mental makeup. It's sort of like the saying, "You can take the boy out of the country, but you can't take the country out of the boy." No matter how far we evolve, we will always possess aggressive and destructive desires; they are not immoral, simply a fact of nature. It is those who refuse to recognize this fact, that proclaim the transcendent morality of man, that are immoral. For it is they who lie to themselves.
>
> Thoreau makes an important step in recognizing the animalistic aspects of human nature. He probably recognized it before he went to Walden Pond but his isolation in the woods enhanced this as a distinct tendency. As he said himself while he lived at the pond he found himself "ranging the woods, like a half starved hound, with strange abandonment, seeking some kind of venison which I might devour." This animalistic instinct became more savage while seeing woodchucks in the woods than it would have if he were in town.
>
> And yet, would he have actually eaten that animal, after just brutally killing it? Of course not. Having never eaten a woodchuck cooked, not to speak of raw, he would be at least reluctant, as civilized humans are when they eat something for the first time. And then,

even before he dipped his finger into the still warm blood, what might be going through his head. Probably, his conscience would be bothering him: "I killed this cute little furry animal for no reason. I'm not even hungry." For civilized animal instincts will always reign over our primitive animal instincts. We are born with a conscience and logical practicality that have made us different from any animal in the forest. Those instincts are so strong, strong enough to prevent the wasteful slaughter of a cute furry friend of the forest.

So it seems that even if we do have a wild and bloodthirsty savage inside of us, the civilized or higher part of our mentality is usually the strongest one, and it manages to fight the urges and desires of the savage inside us quite successfully. This is quite natural: if the savage part of us had remained the stronger one throughout the history of mankind, we would never have become as relatively peaceful and civilized as we are today, and Thoreau would never have been able to write his highly intellectual thoughts on his encounter with a cute furry woodchuck in the forest.

Through facilitating such playful collaborations, word processors can support experiments in adventurous writing. The resultant essays still have lots of rough spots. But they can also provide a model for the ways in which, when students plunge into their writing without knowing exactly where they are going, they sometimes come up with material that is both fun to read and worthy of development.

Building on the various forms of correspondence and collaboration in our classes, many students had begun to expand their communities of discourse by submitting their network entries to campus-wide student publications. We decided to encourage this sort of extension by introducing them to Bitnet, through which they could also share their pieces with freshman writers on other campuses. And, because we found that our students had become proficient at exploring topics of personal interest to themselves and had developed a good sense of what moved their peers as readers, we decided to start challenging their writing skills by suggesting that they now incorporate researched information drawn from primary and secondary sources beyond their usual range of experience. We encourage them to think of "research" as the ability to articulate in their own writing a topic that has already accrued a community of voices discussing it from a variety of angles. By combining networked corresponding with online database searching, we set students to the task of finding appropriate discussions and joining them, and of including within their networked exchanges voices of which they had not previously been aware.

We have found that our students' graded portfolios demonstrate both more risk taking in choice of material and more control over the shaping of that material than we had seen at the end of our previous writing courses. Clearly, this is an anecdotal, rather than quantifiable, finding; it is a report of our evaluations as veteran teachers of writing. Another area in which the impact of networked corresponding was difficult to measure objectively yet impressive to us was in what ENFI Project Director Trent Batson of Gallaudet University describes as "the changes that occur in the classroom environment and, at the same time, changes that occur in the way that students conceive of writing tasks" (1988, p. 55). We found our own roles as teachers changing, first to that of the coach and then to an even more democratized role as we became aware that our voices on the network were not readily distinguishable from the voices of student correspondents. We hoped that our comments, behind which lay years of experience, were sometimes more incisive than peer comments. But we found that students were not waiting for the teacher's word on a piece before they began reworking it. Our role as in-class discussion leaders was changing as well. Because discussions of the readings were taking place before class on the network, we found it necessary to browse the entries and responses first. Then, in class, rather than initiate dialogue we would channel and contribute to what was already an ongoing conversation. We found that their networked corresponding empowered our students to articulate personal agendas in all aspects of their learning. They set the standards for their networked discussions; they found new ways to use the computers; they suggested interesting supplemental readings; and they set their own writing goals in teacher–student conferences where together we planned strategies for achieving them. Sometimes even grading became a subject of dialogue during our final portfolio conferences.

This changed classroom environment is not without its attendant risks. One needs to experience only a single episode of system failure, to stand seemingly helpless in the classroom before a large screen monitor flashing the error message "Bad Interpreter" in order to begin questioning the directions in which computer technology is moving. One can empathize with Wordsworth, the "Pilgrim resolute" early in *The Prelude*, taking "even with the chance equipment of that hour, / The road that pointed toward the chosen Vale" (I, 101–2). But, as we had suspected from the outset, the changes in our students' thinking and writing processes in this new, computerized environment were still consistent with our goals for them as writing teachers. The advantages the computer can offer our students, conscious of its various uses, are fundamentally compatible with the social-constructionist or, as James Berlin has recently called it, "social epistemic" rhetoric with which we are most comfortable (1988, p. 488). What surprised us was the degree to which networked corresponding enhanced our creation of a writing community. There seemed to be an unanticipated dimension added, an energy for which we could not, at the outset, account. It stemmed, we think now, from our discovery ("our" includes teachers and students) of the liberating nature of fluid discourse.

NOTES

1. For a report on our project at an earlier stage, see Kathleen Skubikowski and John Elder, "Word Processing in a Community of Writers," *College Composition and Communication* 38 (May 1987): 198–207.

2. We took as our basic system the model of exploration and correspondence presented in Elder et al. (1989).

3. For a comparison between student writing composed on-screen and text simply typed into the computer, see Diane Pelkus Balestri, "Softcopy and Hard: Wordprocessing and Writing Process," *Academic Computing* (February 1988): 14–17, 41–45.

4. The Musical Computer exercise is more fully described in Elder et al.

WORKS CITED

Batson, Trent. "The ENFI Project: A Networked Classroom Approach to Writing Instruction." *Academic Computing* (February/March 1988): 32–33, 55–56.

Berlin, James. "Rhetoric and Ideology in the Writing Class." *College English* 50 (September 1988): 477–94.

Bruffee, Kenneth A. "Collaborative Learning and the 'Conversation of Mankind.'" *College English* 46 (November 1984): 635–652.

Elbow, Peter. "The Shifting Relationships between Speech and Writing." *College Composition and Communication* 36 (October 1985): 283–303.

Elder, John, Betsy Bowen, Jeffrey Schwartz, and Dixie Goswami. *Word Processing in a Community of Writers* (New York: Garland Publishing, 1989).

Hall, Donald, ed. *The Contemporary Essay* (New York: Bedford/St. Martin's, 1984).

Kemp, Fred. "The User-Friendly Fallacy." *College Composition and Communication* 38 (February 1987): 32–39.

Moffett, James. "Writing, Inner Speech, and Meditation." *College English* 44 (March 1982): 231–246.

Smart, William. *Eight Modern Essayists* (New York: St. Martin's Press, 1985).

Zinsser, William. *On Writing Well* (New York: Harper & Row, 1985).

Computer Conferencing: Composing a Feminist Community of Writers

MARY J. FLORES
Lewis Clark State College

A student in one of my composition courses once explained her earlier frustrations as a high school student to her classmates and me via our class computer conference.[1] She was working on an academic autobiography that I had given the class as an essay assignment. In the conference, she wrote that no matter how often she had requested shop and advanced science courses on her class request forms, the school counselor inevitably put her into home-ec and typing classes. As a result, she hated school because she felt powerless there. Later, in the military, she found she could control the decisions made on her behalf by purposely failing the typing tests to ensure she would not again be routed toward secretarial work. This was the first time she had articulated her experiences with a system that had taught her to act dumb in order to get her way. It was the first time she openly questioned whether her experiences had been unique to her, or replicated in the experiences of other students. It was also the first time she recognized that her education had in some way attempted to silence her. The computer conference gave her the opportunity to voice her experiences and to make connections and understand her experiences in new ways through dialogue with other students.

In the composition class, the computer conference is one method by which we can bring the authority of the student's personal experience into the curriculum, integrating personal experience with received knowledge. We are indeed challenged by the increased availability and use of computers at the university level to use the technology appropriately and effectively. At the same time, current cognitive, pedagogical, and feminist research makes abundantly clear the need for a profound change in the traditional university approach to teaching and learning. It is possible to use computers to preserve and strengthen the institutional status quo, or to use the technology as a means of change—in our approaches to teaching, learning, authority, power, and knowledge.

The institutional status quo favors the dissemination and reception of knowledge through "objectivity," abstraction, hierarchy, and competition. In the traditional lecture presentation of content, the teacher acts as banker/"depositor," as Paulo Freire has argued, making "deposits which the students," acting in this setting as passive "depositories," "patiently receive, memorize, and repeat" (1970, p. 58). Such a model works against women in a number of ways. First, the curriculum itself oppresses them. Written largely by men, about men, and for men, college curricula require women to espouse a male world view. Freire further argues that the banking system of education diminishes students' critical abilities.

> The more students work at storing the deposits entrusted to them, the less they develop the critical consciousness which would result from their intervention in the world as transformers of that world. The more completely they accept the passive role imposed on them, the more they tend simply to adapt to the world as it is and to the fragmented view of reality deposited in them. (p. 60)

Though Freire does not address feminist concerns in his work, Frances Maher points out its relevance to feminists, noting that "this traditional version of education as the wisdom of generations is especially pernicious for women (and other oppressed groups) because its content has often ignored or demeaned them. They are memorizing truths to which their own historical, cultural, and personal experience gives the lie" (1985, p. 30). Thus, while women are memorizing masculine versions of history and culture, feminist experience is effectively silenced.

Women are asked not only to accept a dominant world view that tends to endorse patriarchal authority if they are to succeed at the university, but to speak in the language authorized by that authority as well. As Carol Gilligan persuasively demonstrates in her work on women's moral development, men tend to perceive situations in terms of hierarchy and abstraction, solving a moral problem as an "impersonal conflict of claims" (1982, p. 32). Women, however, tend to perceive situations as a "network of connection, a web of relationships that is sustained by a process of communication" (p. 32). Thus, where men's thinking and expression rely on a competitive framework, women's thinking and expression rely on a collaborative framework. In a traditional classroom setting, therefore, where the method of teaching through lecture and abstraction of facts and empirical evidence is dominant, and where students are encouraged to debate the issues to achieve the "best" answer, many women are alienated and silenced. For these students such a situation can become critical. Either they must allow themselves to be co-opted by the system and become bilingual, as Robin Lakoff (1975) has termed it—putting aside the language they have been taught as children, which focuses on relationships, feelings, and context, and assuming the dominant masculine language of abstraction and objectivity—or they must choose not to speak. We must see this conflict as critical to the university as well. As institutions we seek to empower individuals through education; if we render a portion of our students silent, then we fail to enfranchise them, and we become that much less powerful ourselves.

The widespread adoption of computers as an educational tool gives universities the opportunity for more power than ever before. But we have choices about that power—whether to use it to extend our authority or to empower our students. Nowhere is this situation more evident than in the composition class. Because writing is a social activity—one that establishes a relationship between the writer, the writing, and the reader—we need to establish writing communities in our composition courses. The networking capabilities of computers give us many opportunities to foster such communities, by increasing participation and collaboration and recognizing diversity among our students. A review of the research on computers and composition shows, however, that computers have been used largely as a means to disseminate information more efficiently and to increase our control over students' writing processes and products. In his 1987 bibliographic review of computers and composition, Hugh Burns writes, "The argument that always convinces me that we ought to be active in using the technology as well as we humanly can is simply this: since the machine is already in our garden, let's not be afraid to use it to help us do our jobs more efficiently and, perhaps, effectively" (p. 385). This argument suggests that computers might best be used to expand and increase the ease with which we control our students, not to expand and increase their ease in the classroom, or sense of control over their own educations.

Many programs have been designed to help us be efficient: grammar instruction, individualized programs for checking mechanics, even interactive software—where students interact with computers, not with other writers. Programs have also been designed to teach the writing process, but they make no provision for collaboration or peer response. One computer enthusiast and composition instructor envisions actively involving the teacher in computer-based evaluation and editing by keying the keyboard so that "in evaluating a student's writing on a computer screen we might hit one key and automatically type SUBJ-VERB AGR or TOPIC SENT? or whatever other comments we most commonly make" (Burns, p. 396). In Burns' entire review of computers and composition, even in the section projecting their future together, he does not once mention computer conferencing. Indeed, he argues that the issue for the "motivated, intelligent teacher" will be to "incorporate 'smart' algorithms for representing writing expertise, for capturing writing performance, and intelligently providing the appropriate feedback" (p. 400).

Such approaches to computers and composition threaten to further divorce language from experience, and in so doing, to further alienate our students (especially our women students) from their writing, their peers, and their teachers. The issue for the composition teacher, then, is to use computers to facilitate an interactive, diverse, and collaborative writing community in which every student has a voice and can engage in dialogue with each and every other member of that community. I would never claim that a composition classroom requires a computer conference in order to achieve these goals, since many of us have been striving toward diversity and collaboration through the use of peer groups and other innovative methods. I would argue, however, that the networking capabilities are an important resource that we can use to alter traditional patterns of communication in the classroom and to help our students achieve a greater respect for their own voices, a greater sense of the context of community in composition, and a stronger connection to the community of scholars at the university.

The computer conference can allow for division and difference in ways that are more difficult to achieve in the traditional classroom. The conference gives each individual voice equal access at the same time that it prompts the individual to consider other voices and to acknowledge alternative perspectives. This is not always the case in face-to-face discussions in our classes. Numerous studies have demonstrated that women students often do not have equal opportunity to participate in class discussions or even in small-group discussions. In "The Classroom Climate: Still a Chilly One for Women" (1987), Bernice Sandler lists a variety of "subtle behaviors" displayed by faculty that make full participation in the class more difficult for women than for men, ranging from making eye contact more often with male students than with female students, to asking women "lower-order questions that require factual answers while asking men higher-order questions that demand personal evaluation and critical thinking" (pp. 117–120).

But it's not just a matter of changing faculty behaviors. Studies by Candace West and Don Zimmerman (1983) demonstrate that in conversations between men and women, men interrupt the women 75–96 percent of the time, they interrupt them much more quickly than women interrupt men, and they hold the floor longer. Related studies by Pamela Fishman (1983) seem to indicate that men also choose the topic of conversation almost twice as often as women. Such studies make clear that if we want to incorporate the student's personal experience into the curriculum, and by so doing allow women to use language in familiar ways and still be successful at the university, then we have to change the patterns of communication between men and women students and between faculty and students in the classroom.

Moreover, although this paper focuses specifically on the power of computer conferencing to enfranchise women in the classroom, the computer conference has the power to enfranchise everyone in the class. Many of our students are marginalized and silenced in our classrooms for reasons other than, or in addition to, gender, such as race, culture, educational background, and physical disability. At the first meeting of a composition class for which I planned to use computer conferencing, I stressed to the students that the class would be a workshop and they would all be expected to spend lots of time in class talking to each other. Later that day I found a letter in my office from one of the students in that class. He asked me if I wanted him to drop the course immediately because he would be unable to talk to his classmates. He had a severe stuttering problem. When he came to my office to receive my answer, he was unable to articulate even a single word. Without a computer conference, he would have been relegated to the role of observer of other students' workshop efforts. I was able to assure him, however, that he could be a full participator through the computer conference, and he was. He signed on to the conference every day, sometimes twice a day, and he was a real boost to the system. He had volumes to say and was an experienced "listener" to other students' entries as well. This was his second year at college, and the first class in which he was able to discuss the material with his classmates. He had previously avoided courses that emphasized discussion, but when the semester ended, he enrolled in a literature course that also used computer conferencing.

Although this student's active participation in discussion occurred mostly outside the classroom, his participation in the conference nevertheless changed his participation in the classroom. Students would comment in class on his latest entries in the conference; they were more comfortable talking to him since they knew him better through their computer conversations; he was an equal participant in peer-group work through his fuller integration into the classroom community.

The computer conference facilitates changes in classroom dynamics by modeling a more egalitarian mode of dialogue.[2] Each student has equal access to the conference. Each student has an equal opportunity to introduce topics for discussion and to respond to topics. Each student can "hold the floor" as long as she or he chooses and cannot be interrupted. The lines of dialogue can fan out, weblike, from one student to many; between two students or a few; or round robin to all conference members, rather than just from student to teacher and vice versa. The forms of dialogue might vary from question and answer to topic and comment, to analysis, debate, reflection, and shared experience.

Shared-experience discussions are a critical feature of the computer conference. The brief narrative that opens this paper is an example of one such discussion on a computer conference.[3] This student asked others in the conference if they had had similar experiences in school and, if so, how they had handled them. The responses were many and varied. Some students had experienced similar frustrations but had not before labeled them as gender stereotyping or perceived a pattern to their experiences until they saw them mirrored in their peers' backgrounds as well. Some men entered experiences about the pressures they had felt in school to perform athletically. A few who hadn't participated in competitive sports said they had felt that they had to compensate for that deficit by "overachieving" scholastically or artistically.

Students do not normally have an opportunity to share these kinds of experiences in their classes. They do not have the opportunity because, first, as I have argued above, traditional classroom dynamics discourage this kind of open-ended discussion. Second, we often feel we have too much to do in meeting specific curriculum objectives and content to give class time up to extended discussion. Third, and perhaps most importantly, the institution has not valued the individual's experience, especially women's experience, as objective, valid data.

These shared-experience discussions, however, can lead to vital, political writing that firmly locates the writer's experience as part of the process by which she or he constructs knowledge. Moreover, it leads to writing that recognizes alternative experiences and, thus, alternative conclusions and values. Pamela Annas argues that

> because historically women have been channeled toward private forms and denied access to more public forms, it has seemed to me particularly important to teach women how to write political essays—by which I mean any essay that places the self in the world, is addressed to an audience, and takes a position. (1985, p. 369)

Two students involved in the computer conference discussion on high school experiences eventually wrote just that kind of political essay. After completing her academic autobiography, the woman who initiated the conference item went on to write an argumentative essay on how schools harm students when they take control away from them, using her own experience as the basis for her position. Another student went on to consider the negative effects of competition on adolescents, drawing on resources in the computer discussion and integrating personal experience with external authority.

A third student came to reconsider his initial argument that the grading system is an impartial assessment of students' achievements. He argued that high marks should be given only to those students who produce the best work because all students have equal opportunity to produce equal results. Through the process of discussing these issues with his peers on the conference, however, he came to a greater appreciation of the complexity of the grading system. One student told him about the C she received for an art project because she had refused to change her project to please the instructor. She felt what she had accomplished in that project was superior to anything else she'd ever produced. Other students told him about the A's they had received for work they considered to have little merit. Students questioned his premise that all students have equal opportunities in the public school system. Some students, one class member pointed out, have enough money to go to school full-time and devote all their energies to studying and achieving top grades; others work full-time to be able to afford tuition and books. The student who initiated this topic wrote a first paper in which he expressed his clear views supporting tough, objective grading standards. In his second paper he floundered, waivering between attempts to establish some objective criteria for grading and to do justice to the experiences of his classmates. In his third paper he used the problems he had encountered as the basis of his writing. He still felt that there had to be some means of evaluating and validating the relative worth of students' work, but he now argued that we needed to understand much more about the differences among students before we could establish such a system.

Although not all students went on to write papers drawn as directly as these from the conference discussions, some did use the discussions for topic invention, recognizing those issues that elicited strong responses from peers as important topics to address in more formal writing. For instance, one of the discussions on the conference concerned students' views on whether the primary purpose of the university was to provide job training to students or a liberal arts education. Most students said the university should give a graduate a well-rounded education, but it should also help them get a job. One student asked the others if they would stay in school if they felt absolutely sure that they would earn no more money with a degree than without. Many did not respond to this question, but one woman did. As a dance major, she said, she was just marking time in school until she got into a good company. She would drop everything in a minute for a job because a degree could not possibly help her. She went on to design a portfolio project that explored the value of a university education to an artist. This conference discussion generated another discussion that focused on defining a "well-rounded" education. Another student developed her own criteria for a well-rounded education and wrote a rationale for her choices.

Although shared-experience discussions on the computer conference may begin at the prewriting or invention stage of the composing process, they have the potential to go beyond that function and alter students' writing by strengthening their sense of connection to their own texts and to their readers. In *Women's Ways of Knowing* (1986), Mary Belenky and her colleagues argue that women students need to learn to integrate personal and public voices at a position of "constructed knowledge." Women perceive themselves and the world, they argue, either from a position of "received knowledge and procedural knowledge," where they rely on such external factors as authority, texts, institutions, and traditional roles for understanding and identity, or from a position of "subjective knowledge," where they have a strong sense of personal truth, but little regard for other voices and limited ability to articulate their private truths to others (p. 134). The constructivist, however, recognizes that "all knowledge is constructed, and the knower is an intimate part of the known" (p. 137). Such students are able to participate fully in their educations, as they are able to articulate what they have learned through experience and make connections with the knowledge and experiences of others.

Students who participate in a computer conference with their peers over the course of a semester begin to move toward a constructivist approach to writing and thinking. They arrive at, or approach, this position because an open-ended, student-centered conference enables students to make personal connections to, and digressions from, the topics at hand. Moreover, it enables them to see connections and differences between their experiences and the experiences of their peers. Through the recognition of sameness and difference, a student comes to recognize the value of her or his own voice—as the voice that shares and strengthens the common experience, or the voice that tests and casts doubt on generalizations and argues for a new, or broader, understanding. These students approach writing and learning as a dynamic activity, involving a network of personal background and experience, peer response, and external authority.

Most colleges and universities are introducing, if not increasing the use of, computers. As we become more and more adept at using the technology, we must find applications that empower all our students to speak. If we use computer-conferencing capabilities to teach our students to approach writing and learning from a position of authority, then we are also enfranchising them as members of the community of scholars that comprise the university. Through their involvement in a computer conference and other collaborative activities, and subsequently through their writing, our students can go beyond information retrieval and delivery. They can reciprocate the knowledge and experience we share with them with their own insights, challenging and changing our own ways of thinking and writing.

N O T E S

1. I used a computer conference for several sections of Intensive Composition at the University of Michigan–Ann Arbor between 1986 and 1987. In these courses, students designed a writing portfolio on an educational issue. I am grateful to the University of Michigan for the opportunity to use the computer conference in my courses.

2. Also see Chapter 7 of this book, Cynthia Selfe's "Technology in the English Classroom: Computers through the Lens of Feminist Theory," for an additional explanation of the ways computer conferences can change classroom dynamics.

3. In addition to shared-experience discussions, there are many other ways I use a computer conference, including revision work, collaborative writing, providing feedback on drafts, extending class discussion on readings, and private conversations between me and students regarding their writing or their participation in class.

W O R K S   C I T E D

Annas, Pamela J. "Style as Politics: A Feminist Approach to the Teaching of Writing." *College English* 47, no. 4 (1985): 360–371.

Belenky, Mary Field, et al. *Women's Ways of Knowing: The Development of Self, Voice, and Mind.* New York: Basic Books, 1986.

Burns, Hugh. "Computers and Composition." *Teaching Composition: 12 Bibliographical Essays.* Ed. Gary Tate. Fort Worth: Texas Christian University, 1987, pp. 378–400.

Fishman, Pamela M. "Interaction: The Work Women Do." *Language, Gender, and Society.* Ed. B. Thorne, C. Kramarea, and N. Henley. Rowley, MA: Newbury House, 1983, pp. 89–101.

Freire, Paulo. *Pedagogy of the Oppressed.* Trans. Myra Bergman Ramos. New York: Seabury Press, 1970.

Gilligan, Carol. *In a Different Voice: Psychological Theory and Women's Development.* Cambridge, MA: Harvard, 1982.

Lakoff, Robin. *Language and Woman's Place.* New York: Harper & Row, 1975.

Maher, Frances. "Classroom Pedagogy and the New Scholarship on Women." *Gendered Subjects: The Dynamics of Feminist Teaching.* Ed. Margo Culley and Catherine Portuges. Boston: Routledge & Kegan Paul, 1985, pp. 29–48.

Sandler, Bernice Resnick. "The Classroom Climate: Still a Chilly One for Women." *Educating Men and Women Together: Coeducation in a Changing World.* Ed. Carol Lasser. Urbana: The University of Illinois, 1987, pp. 113–123.

West, Candace, and Don H. Zimmerman. "Small Insults: A Study of Interruptions in Cross-Sex Conversations between Unacquainted Persons." *Language, Gender, and Society.* Ed. B. Thorne, C. Kramarae, and N. Henley. Rowley, MA: Newbury House, 1983, pp. 102–117.

Technology in the English Classroom: Computers through the Lens of Feminist Theory

CYNTHIA L. SELFE
Michigan Technological University

Computers are powerful tools for generating, exchanging, and accessing written information. These machines, English composition teachers have learned, change the nature of written communication and, thus, the nature of literacy education itself. But, if we have come to recognize some of the far-reaching effects of computers, we have done far less to interpret these effects in light of the theoretical perspectives that inform our teaching of reading and writing. To date, the bulk of our profession's work with computer technology has been anecdotal and observational rather than theoretical or explanatory in any broader philosophical, social, or rhetorical sense.

THE PROBLEM: A NEED FOR THEORETICAL PERSPECTIVE

Historically, there is good reason for our limited theoretical work in connection with computers and their use in literacy programs. Our work with computers is still in its infancy. And, as happens in most youthful fields of inquiry, preliminary explorations first take the form of isolated experiments or practical applications of the technology that are ungrounded in a broader understanding of principle. However, although such pioneering work is *necessary* in beginning the exploration of a new field, it is also *limited* in scope and perspective. Because such work is preliminary and exploratory in nature, it does not serve to establish critical, interdisciplinary perspectives or to inform in any systematic way our educational practices. As Greg Meyers notes, "Without an awareness of . . . theories, we can neither address other teaching practices, nor criticize our own" (1987, p. 213).

Our atheoretical approach to computer use, for example, has assured that teachers' experiences with technology in the English classroom remain mostly unconnected with broader language and communication concepts, or with broader interpretations of social and historical concerns. As a result, those findings we *have* obtained about how computers affect writing and reading processes are difficult to generalize (Hawisher 1986) and limited in their usefulness for teachers in other academic and sociopolitical situations.

This atheoretical perspective, from which only rare scholars like Janet Eldred (1989) or Richard Ohmann (1985) have deviated, not only constrains our current educational uses of computers, but also seriously limits our vision of what might be accomplished with computer technology in a broader social, cultural, or educational context. Until we examine the impact of computer technology on language and society from a theoretical perspective, we will continue, myopically and unsystematically, to define isolated pieces of the puzzle in our separate classrooms and discrete research studies. Until we share some theoretical vision of this topic, we will never glimpse the larger social or educational picture that could give our everyday classroom efforts direction and meaning. "Theory," Marilyn Cooper reminds us, "is prior to, and essential to, good practice" (1987, p. 1).

Perhaps even more important, however, we know as a profession that theoretical examination contributes centrally to making our discipline intellectually responsible in a broad social and cultural sense. And it may be this contribution that speaks most dramatically to those of us who study computer use within reading- and writing-intensive classrooms. In a 1987 *Profession 87* article, Cary Nelson notes,

. . . only a theorized discipline can be an effective site for a general social critique—that is, a discipline actively engaged in self-criticism, a discipline that is a locus for struggle, a discipline that renews and revises its awareness of history, a discipline that inquires into its differential relations with other academic fields, and a discipline that examines its place in the social formation and is willing to adapt its . . . practices to suit different social functions. (p. 48)

Scholars in the field of computers and composition have recently come to recognize the role of theory in establishing a critical and contextual vision of a field, especially within a social, political, or historical framework. And as they have done so, they have also come to accept that there is a challenging task ahead of them—that of grounding our profession's understanding of technology in existing theoretical frameworks so that we may better understand the potential of technology as a force in literacy education.

The remainder of this chapter represents one contribution to this effort. The discussion that follows is an attempt to theorize about computer use in reading- and writing-intensive classes: first, by constructing an alternative, theoretically based vision of computer technology; and second, by demonstrating how such a perspective might be used to modify, in a positive sense, our own and our students' notions of literacy. The aim of constructing this alternative vision is to question the status quo, our current academic system that extends privilege—for various historical, social, and economic reasons—to competitive individual work over collaborative group work; to power over weakness; to men over women; to science over the humanities; to tradition over change. This system of privilege is not only supported by computer technology, but enhanced by it.

In contrast, an alternative vision of computer use may help us understand how to extend privilege to communication over isolation, collaboration over competition, and change over tradition. Technology, in this vision, can help our profession provide wider and more egalitarian access to reading and writing communities via computer networks, ensure our students increasingly active and collaborative engagements with discourse and text, and broaden our traditional notions of unnegotiated, one-way power relationships between writers and readers. From such an exercise, we can also learn that the value of computers in our classrooms is due as much to their power as tools for social and political reform of literacy education as it is to their power as tools of communication.

As a theoretical lens in this effort, I have chosen to employ feminist theory because it facilitates the political activity of creating radically alternative visions or perspectives. In considering the uses of computer technology, feminist theory allows us to look critically at the context of what we now know, of how we currently use and see computers, in order to rethink the relationship between techno/power and literacy and then reconstruct the role computers could play in our literacy efforts.[1] In this way, feminist theory can help us give form, shape, and vision to our future uses of computers.

In particular, the discussion that follows is informed by the theoretical perspective of "liberal" feminism. "Liberal" feminism shares with "radical" and "Marxist/socialist" feminism the recognition that women (and other minorities) have traditionally been and continue to be devalued, oppressed, and silenced, but it recognizes the possibility of modifying existing political, social, and economic structures to promote and support equity in opportunity.[2]

Working from this "liberal" feminist perspective, the discussion that follows places a positive value on

1. The opportunity for egalitarian participation in and influence on social, political, and economic contexts.
2. The opportunity to reconstruct such contexts so that egalitarian participation is possible.
3. The opportunity to engage in and be central to conversations or text exchanges within these contexts.
4. The opportunity to negotiate or reinterpret the form and meaning of texts within alternative linguistic contexts.[3]

These assumptions, shaped broadly by the thinking of feminist scholars from a range of political perspectives, suggest educational contexts and classroom settings that turn "outsiders" into "insiders" (Gornick 1971); that are broadly inclusive and embracing, nonhierarchical, student-centered communities (Rabinowitz 1983;

Mielke 1987; Quinn 1987); and that encourage the opportunity for active and equal involvement of individuals in making personal and political decisions of all kinds (Wittig 1969; Firestone 1971).

Such classrooms would value personal and group discovery through open discussion, collaboration, and process-based writing and reading activities (Gilligan 1982; Reinharz 1983; Däumer and Runzo 1987; Perry 1987). Within these educational settings, teachers and students would recognize the benefits of multiple "voices" and perspectives (Wittig 1969; Gilligan 1982); and the advantages of experimenting with language (Miller and Swift 1976; Nilsen et al. 1977; Rich 1979; Spender 1980) and political/ pedagogical structures (Sargent 1974; Caywood and Overing 1987). Classrooms informed by feminist theory would also value attention to alternative, noncanonical literature and interpretation (Sargent 1974; Patraka 1983; Däumer and Runzo 1987; Frey 1987).

FEMINIST THEORY AND COMPUTERS

So what kind of a vision of computers can we get if we look through the lens of liberal feminist theory; and, perhaps more importantly, how can this vision shape the ways in which we integrate computers into our reading- and writing-intensive class-rooms? We can begin with a general picture, the various parts of which will be covered in more specific detail during the discussion that follows. Within reading- and writing-intensive classrooms, computer networks, computer conferences, and computer-based text production can help us demarginalize those individuals who have been excluded from our discussions by more traditional approaches to the teaching of literacy. Such systems can, in a feminist sense, invite more people into active engagements with, and conversations about, texts and encourage them to participate in different, and perhaps more egalitarian, ways than might be possible using more traditional media. In addition, computers may help us broaden our notions of authorship, readership, and interpretation and, thus, change our ideas about traditionally privileged texts.

1. *Inviting more people into active discussions of texts and into conversations about these texts*

One of the most tantalizing things we have learned about computer-mediated communication in the past few years is that meetings via computer networks encourage more people to participate in group discussions and efforts than do similarly constructed face-to-face meetings (Kiesler et al. 1984; Fersko-Weiss 1985; Pfaffenberger 1986; Pullinger 1986; Spitzer 1989). Specifically, computer networks encourage increased participation and exchange by accomplishing two things: first, by making it possible for individuals who might otherwise be prevented from contributing to a discussion to do so; and second, by facilitating conversations within dialogic groups that would otherwise find such conversations so cumbersome or slow as to be less than worthwhile at all.

Several kinds of research projects have contributed to our understanding of this phenomenon. Studies grounded in technology applications, for instance, indicate that computer networks make conversations possible for writers and readers who live in different geographical locations (Pfaffenberger 1986; Holvig 1987; Spitzer 1989); for individuals who are handicapped ("Computer Talks" 1988) or do not find it possible, because of age or economic constraints (Holvig 1987; Ludtke 1987), to get to a traditional classroom where they can participate in academic conversations; and for individuals who do not find the traditional classroom a conducive environment for contributing to intellectual discussion (Hiltz 1986).

If we look at these findings through the lens of feminist theory, we can see the value of computer networks within any reading- or writing-intensive classroom. Given the right circumstances (and by this I mean the right software and hardware systems along with the money to make them work), computer networks can make it possible for individual writers and readers who have been prevented from entering our academic conversations in the past to become central contributors. In this vision, computer networks become human networks—electronic circles that support alternative, nontraditional dialogue and dialectic, communities that value revision and reinterpretation of traditional educational structures.[4]

Given the constraints of our current academic system, which is detailed in the next section, such inclusive involvement cannot take place in a traditional classroom but might be supported within a computer-supported one—a virtual classroom, for instance, that exists only within a computer system, or on a computer network that supplements a traditional writing classroom (Selfe and Wahlstrom 1989).

Research completed within the field of composition assures us that such a vision is not an impractical one. Individual scholars have used computers and computer networks to promote collaborative exchanges among colleagues within academic professions (Bernhardt and Appleby 1985; Pfaffenberger 1986; Pullinger 1986), among teachers of writing and their students (Selfe and Wahlstrom 1985), and among groups of students engaged in writing- and reading-intensive tasks (Daiute 1985; Rodrigues 1985; Selfe and Eilola 1988).

Even now, computer networks are encouraging electronic discourse communities to form and to exchange information as readers and writers. And many of these communities would not or could not have formed in traditional classrooms. BreadNet students in a suburb of New York, for example, are using a computer network to communicate with their peers on an Indian reservation in South Dakota (Bowen and Schwartz 1986; Holmsten 1987). Deaf students at Gallaudet University are using a computer network in their English classes to converse in "real time" with their peers and their teachers (Batson 1988); and at the New York Institute of Technology, more than 200 university students living in remote locations attend classes on an electronic, computer-based network (Spitzer 1989).[5]

2. *Encouraging more active and more egalitarian participation within academic conversations based on reading and writing*

Although increased participation and collaboration are desirable aspects of computer use, they are not all that we might want for our alternative vision of computers within reading- and writing-intensive classrooms. Instead, influenced by feminist theory, we would also want to ensure that increased participation on computer networks or within a computer-supported classroom can, in turn, encourage new, different, even revolutionary *patterns* of information exchange and conversations—those that allow individuals with traditionally marginal relationships to an academic discourse community to bring themselves to the center of that community's exchanges.

Research findings support the possibility of such alternative patterns' existing within computer-supported environments. During the past five years, for instance, social psychologists have noted that individuals who communicate via computer networks, because they are not conducting face-to-face conversations, are free to eliminate or ignore many of the social/hierarchical cues that mark traditional exchanges—cues associated with gender, race, position in established organizational hierarchies, social status, or appearance (Spitzer 1986). This ability to minimize social/hierarchical cues, in turn, can contribute to increasingly egalitarian participation by individual group members engaged in a common task and decreasing the potential for group domination by individuals (Kiesler et al. 1984).

Still other studies indicate that computers facilitate communicative exchanges and discussions by altering the political relationships existing within traditional classrooms. The use of computer networks in a writing classroom situation, for instance, often seems to shift focus from the teachers to the students, prompting more discussion that is student-centered (Daiute 1985; Selfe and Wahlstrom 1985; Hiltz 1986).

I recently had occasion to observe just how dramatically the use of computer technology can affect students and their intellectual exchanges in a writing-intensive class. The class, which I taught earlier this year, proved to be a perfect observational laboratory for my purposes because it was conducted in two very different settings: one traditional and one electronic. In the traditional classroom sessions, the students and I met twice a week to discuss their readings and their interpretations of texts. We also met twice a week, however, in an electronic environment. Everyone in the class, including me, contributed to an electronic conference in which we discussed our responses to the issues we cover during class sessions. This conversation took place on a computer network in Michigan Tech's computer-supported writing lab. Class members could contribute to the dialogue whenever they wanted, as long as they did so at least once a week, and they could use pseudonyms if they wished. The patterns of conversation and interpretation that existed in these two environments, that of the traditional classroom and that of the electronic classroom, differed widely.

In the former setting, although I tried my best to keep my mouth shut, to minimize the traditional threat of grading, to downplay my role as teacher, and to support students' contributions, patterns of dialogue and exchange were still basically traditional. When I talked, they listened; my very presence was a constant visual reminder that I was different from them. I was older than they were; I dressed differently than most of them did; I was wealthier and had a different relationship with my colleagues than they did. Even though we sat in a circle to disguise the fact that we were different in status, my presence and contributions were privileged in such a traditional setting, and there was little I could do about this situation.

These facts—that this was a class, that I was a teacher, and that discussions were ultimately graded—also made my students react in predictable ways. Those who were more verbally articulate about their knowledge of the readings were rewarded by smiles and nods from other students, and by my attention. Those who were more assertive about their views got more rewards. As a result of this situation, whether I wanted it to happen or not, some students were silenced and oppressed. Women, who traditionally speak less than men (Rich 1979; Spender 1980) and are interrupted more often (Zimmerman and West 1975), were at a disadvantage, as were students who were less articulate in oral than in written discourse. Students who wanted to take time to think about their response before they offered it or students who were merely polite were also mostly out of luck. The discussion in the traditional classroom sessions tended to proceed at a breakneck pace and, sometimes, in a competitive manner. Older students, who may have been hesitant to add their views, or students with handicaps and who could not verbalize would also have been disadvantaged in such a setting.[6]

In the electronic environment, all of these things changed. Because I employed a pseudonym much of the time, my contributions to the conversation were frequently unmarked by my role as teacher and were treated like those of any other participant. The lack of face-to-face cues in the conference meant that gender, age, and social status also disappeared except as individuals chose to reveal themselves by bringing specific experiences into their written responses. What counted in such a setting, as Michael Spitzer (1989) has observed, is the quality of a student's thinking. What was said became more important, at least for a moment, than who said it.

From what I can tell after my experiences with several of these electronic conferences, discussions of texts are frequently more freewheeling than those held in traditional classroom settings, given the lack of normal turn-taking rules; longer, given the ease of keyboarding and revising on the computer; and more emotion-laden to compensate for the lack of face-to-face paralinguistic cues.

In the electronic environment of my class, those quieter members and those who wanted to mull over their responses before they contributed were no longer silenced or marginal in our discussions. They spoke as loudly, as articulately, and as frequently as anyone else.

I am not suggesting that this electronic "conference" represents the only direction in which we can or should move with regard to our computer use in writing- or reading-intensive classes, but I do believe it represents a healthy complement to the traditional classroom, one in which we can promote more egalitarian discussion and provide marginal community members a medium through which their contributions might become increasingly central.

In a broader educational context, it may be that such environments can offer marginalized groups a forum in which to rediscover their own voice, to reinterpret and reconstruct their experience, and to make meaning that reflects their own cultural and intellectual contributions.[7] And this forum, in turn, may help transform the composition classroom into increasingly effective environments which, as Elisabeth Däumer and Sandra Runzo advocate, "enable students to find a voice to combat the pervasive forces in our culture that silence women and others, who because of race, class, or other circumstances have been permitted less visibility and whose concerns have been suppressed . . ." (1987, p. 53).

3. *Broadening notions of authorship, readership, interpretation, and privilege in connection with texts*

Finally, I'd like to point out one more area in which feminist theory can profitably inform the directions in which we move to integrate computers into our classes. This involves our vision of authorship, readership, and interpretation of written texts. To understand the impact of computers on such issues, however, we must first recognize what it means to make text electronic.

Computers, from what we have been able to tell, change our very notion of text. There are grammars involved in reading, writing, and manipulating text on a computer screen that make us see these activities differently from the ways we do when they are manifested on a printed page (Selfe 1987). On a computer screen, text is more fluid than it is on a page, as James Catano (1985) points out, because we can change the word so easily. On a screen, a text becomes dynamic in every sense, from the formation of phosphorescent letters and the rapid movement through a text, to the communication of this text in the blink of an eye over great distances and geographic boundaries.

Psychologically and philosophically, our experiences with this dynamic, mutable quality of computer-supported text alters the ways in which we see and interpret all texts and their relationships with readers. Readers of traditional page-bound text have been trained to see them as fixed entities—books, articles, documents that are shown to us in classroom after classroom in the same form—that we pass down to our students and our children, that we study and gloss and analyze. Readers of electronic text have a dramatically different sense of empowerment in connection with text: To them, text is both changing and changeable (Heim 1987; Lanham 1987).

This fundamental shift in our notion of the fixed, authoritative text is most important. We have heretofore existed, as Richard Lanham notes, in a "one-way hierarchical relationship with what we read," a "master–slave relationship" (1987, p. 4) promoted by the use of fixed texts, and often a fixed canon, in which our commentary on a text—our criticism, our explanation—elicits no changes in the text itself.

In contrast, on a computer screen, text is so mutable that it invites change, lends itself to a new kind of asynchronous, two-directional making of meaning in which both writers and readers can change the shape of ideas with relative ease. The psychological impact of this vision of text is far-reaching in literacy studies and has affected our view of literary texts as well as of student-produced texts. The ease with which text is manipulated by computers has inspired a whole new genre of interactive fiction— programs like *A Mind Forever Voyaging*, *Zork*, and *Hitchhiker's Guide to the Universe*—in which readers discard the traditional role assigned them by page-bound fiction for the chance to be both story-reader and story-shaper, simultaneously.

Certainly, when we consider this situation from the perspective of feminist theory, we can see that computers have the potential for dramatically altering our approach to reading, writing, and interpreting texts in English classrooms. If page-bound texts are associated with one-way, hierarchical exchanges of knowledge and support of a fixed canon (Caywood and Overing 1987; Lanham 1987), which are phallocentrically determined in our culture, then electronic text invites multidirectional, multivoiced exchanges and products.[8]

Writing text in a computer-supported environment, for example, can facilitate certain kinds of collaborative efforts that may not always be possible within the more traditional forums of a regular classroom space. Page-bound readers in our current classrooms are limited in their collaborative writing and reading activity by the traditional ethical boundaries of authorship and ownership; they are forced to interpret fixed texts within the framework of the dominant phallocentric paradigm: our classrooms, our academic conversations, and the fixed texts students themselves produce. They comment on and gloss texts, but they do not change them (Lanham 1987).

Readers in computer-supported classrooms, on the other hand, may not be bound in the same way. In a fundamental sense, the alternative electronic environment in which they work could empower them to re-author text, to reinterpret it in the most radical way: to re-vision, reformat, and rewrite—and all of this in a context where texts, classrooms, and academic conversations need not be controlled by the dominant ideology.

And, although it is extremely difficult to picture a situation that is only beginning to emerge, readers who grow up functioning within such electronic environments may well come to find traditional texts, as Lanham suggests, "awkward to hold and to read, literally colorless . . . , gummous and intractable, resisting any kind of manipulation" (1987, p. 7). Electronic environments that serve as a supplement to the traditional classroom may give these readers the opportunity to deconstruct, in an electronic sense, traditional texts; to radically change our print-based notion of text as that interpretive space in which the author alone makes meaning.

In these senses, computer-supported writing classrooms may help us learn, in a dramatic and physical sense, what it means for literacy education when electronic texts become continually changing collections of meaning negotiated and reinterpreted in collaborative ventures by different sets of author/readers. Even now, teachers who work in computer-supported writing labs and classrooms are coming up against new notions of electronically shared and constructed texts, trying to sort out what belongs to whom and when, as students invent new forms of authorship, collaboration, and production faster than we can identify and name them.

I'm not suggesting that we should all run out tomorrow to discard our current, traditionally determined definitions of authorship, ownership, and interpretation in a frenzy of electronic liberation. That would be absurd, destructive, and probably impossible. Instead, I suggest that we take a peek at this vision or, as Adrienne Rich (1979) might call it, this "re-vision"; that we start supporting alternative electronic environments in our English classes at all levels so that we and our students can begin to explore the limits of electronic interpretation or deconstruction with a freedom denied us in strictly traditional classrooms.

A STATE OF THE STATE ADDRESS

So how does our new vision of educational computer use compare to our current system when we shine the light of liberal feminist theory on both of them? Certainly, the new vision is characterized by a healthy increase in connection, among both humans and machines.

Computer networks, in our feminist vision of technology, serve as an electronic metaphor for "networking" among humans; and the electronic conferences created on these networked systems become forums for the exchange of information, for discussions among individual scholars in a range of educational and geographic settings. Given the support of such systems, for instance, students in Newark, Kalamazoo, Austin, Orlando, and Mexico City may be able to strike up intellectual conversations never before possible, meeting together each week as an electronically supported Jane Austen reading group. Or an advanced French student in a one-room schoolhouse in Copper Harbor, Michigan, may find herself able to join a class at The University of Iowa to read *Madame Bovary* in an early manuscript version.

Unfortunately, although these scenarios are already possible, in a technological sense they are not happening. Connection, although central to a feminist vision of education, is not a characteristic we can use to accurately describe most educational computing systems we now have available to us as teachers. Indeed, our current educational computer systems are characterized by communication problems rather than communication exchange. Evidence to support this statement is too widespread to be coincidental. Although there are some shining exceptions, most elementary and secondary school teachers and students now use computers that cannot "talk" to one another because the machines literally "stand alone" in the back of a classroom or in a lab setting. School boards and administrators, privileging individual achievement over group communication, will pay for computers, but not the essential software and cables needed to link them together.

And school administrators are not the only ones who buy into phallocentric myths of individualistic effort and isolated scholarship—try software and hardware companies. In colleges and universities, English teachers who use computers and have access to networks remain cut off from electronic communication exchanges because they lack the technical expertise, the time, or even the sheer patience needed to decipher opaque and confusing systems. Moreover, those scholars who persevere and learn to use one network may find it impossible to talk to those who use some other network; Bitnet users get lost on their way to EDUCOM because those designing, building, and buying computer equipment have not emphasized connection or transparent communication. Until we, as educational consumers, insist on such connection, the computer companies will continue to produce machines that don't talk to one another, and the schools will continue to buy networking programs that limit access rather than enhance communication.

But if the term *connection* is important to our new vision of educational computer use, so also is the term *alternative*. When English teachers allow students to contribute to conversations about texts and discourse in electronic forums as well as in classroom discussions, they provide the important opportunity for alternative conversations in which communication can take place under some different social and cultural rules than those that limit our current educational system.

And although these forums certainly have their own problems, including electronic plagiarism and eavesdropping, they can, if constructed carefully, offer a place in which students can try out ideas without having to fight the same battles of agism, sexism, and racism that they fight in traditional classroom forums. Computer conferences, as communication environments characterized by reduced risk, may offer some of our traditionally silenced and marginalized students the opportunity to find a voice and to use it effectively in group discussions and conversations. Currently, of course, our educational system allows few enough opportunities for such exchanges.

A third characteristic of our new vision of computer use hinges on the word *equity*: equity of access, equity of participation, and equity of opportunity. The connected, networked system sketched in this paper will work only when oppressed and marginal members of our society have access to computers, to the training required to use this equipment, and to the networks that tie human beings together in a rich web of discourse and exchange.

And, although it is clear that such equity is possible, it is not yet probable. We all know about the "not probable" part. Poor schools have fewer computers than wealthy schools, and poor children fewer computers than rich ones. Children of color, handicapped children, young women, geographically isolated students, and inner-city students may also experience the inequitable distribution of computer resources. Until we change the social and political make-up of this country, these facts remain constants in our lives.[9]

So what about the possibility of equity? Although the falling cost of computers, competition from foreign markets, and the continuing miniaturization of microprocessors give us some hope, the increasing savvy of the computer retail industry provides us even more. With computers becoming less expensive, more sophisticated, and more portable, it is possible to obtain excellent word-processing and networking capabilities for very little money. Both schools and computer vendors, recognizing the potential to boost their share of the market, have teamed up to provide innovative pricing schedules, equipment grants, and computer lending schemes that have made computers accessible to more students than ever before.

A few English teachers have begun to take advantage of this situation to provide their students access to computers and electronically supported discourse communities. Linda Stine (1986) of Lincoln University, for instance, teaches a composition course for nontraditional students in which each individual is given a "loaner" computer for the entire semester.

David Humphreys (1988) of Cuyahoga Community College

provides a similar service for local teachers who enroll in his graduate-level class on computer literacy for English teachers. I would hope that school and public libraries are instituting comparable computer check-out or loan procedures for individuals in other settings.

Among the advantages of looking at a subject through a theoretical lens or from a theoretical perspective is the activity of rethinking and reseeing texts, discourse, and conversations as well as the social/political/historical contexts within which these exchanges exist. In the specific case of feminist theory, this re-vision results from bringing hitherto marginal interpretations to the center of a discussion, teaching readers and writers to make meaning from the lacunae that characterize existing texts and discourse, and letting readers and writers discover the power of active involvement so they can make meaning from texts in their own voices.

In the broadest sense, I believe these values of feminist theory can help us construct a positive and liberating vision of computer use in reading- and writing-intensive classrooms: one in which we can use technology to invite increasing numbers of people into active and more egalitarian discussions of making and interpreting meaning—especially those individuals who have until this point played only a marginal role in such discussions. In addition, I think the perspective of feminist theory can help us adjust to the changes that technology brings to the concept of privileged texts and readers' and writers' relationships with these texts.[10]

If we use computers to accomplish these ends, then we can inspire computer "revolution" of the most meaningful kind—not one concerned with hardware and software, but one concerned with people, education, and liberation.

NOTES

1. I am indebted to *The Techno/Peasant Survival Manual*, for the concept, definition, and discussion of techno/power, techno/peasant, and techno/crat.

2. These distinctions are made and explored thoroughly by H. Leslie Steeves (1987).

3. I have taken the liberty here of stating these tenets in gender-neutral terms. Although women are obviously the focus of feminist theory, this chapter seeks changes in our use of computer technology on behalf of all individuals who participate in our current educational system: all races and nationalities, all economic classes, all religions, and both genders. Thus, the values inherent in liberal feminist theory are used in this paper to inform the shape of suggested reforms, but not to limit the extent of their benefits or applications.

4. These electronic networks suggest Monique Wittig's symbol of "the ring, the O, the zero, the sphere . . ." (1969, p. 45) which is "without limit" and whose "center is everywhere, circumference nowhere" (p. 69). This circle, as Wittig notes, "configures every possible revolution" (p. 69) and is driven by "thousands of voices" (p. 86).

5. For a discussion of how four major universities or educational services offer systematic instruction via computer network, see Brock Meek (1987).

6. For a thorough discussion of how we, as writing teachers, consciously and unconsciously silence and oppress students in composition classrooms, see Cynthia Caywood and Gillian Overing (1987).

7. Adrienne Rich notes that women (and, I can add, other oppressed minorities) will find their voices when "they begin to move out toward what the feminist philosopher Mary Daly terms a 'new space' on the boundaries of patriarchy" (1979, p. 49). Computer networks may provide such spaces—electronic and cultural "lacunae" (Wittig 1969)—in which we learn to listen to multiple voices and, thus, in Carol Gilligan's words, learn the importance of "different truths" (1982, p. 156). In these spaces we may be able to recapture, from women and other "silenced" (Olsen 1978) minorities, perspectives that we have lost.

If computer networks encourage increased egalitarian dialogue in educational settings, as we have suggested, they are indeed revolutionary tools, and not only from a feminist viewpoint. As Paulo Freire (1968) points out, "through dialogue, the teacher-of-the-students and the students-of-the-teacher cease to exist and a new term emerges: teacher-student with students-teachers. . . . They become jointly responsible for a process in which all grow. In this process, arguments based on 'authority' are no longer valid . . ." (p. 67). This active and frank dialogue, Freire continues, supports an increasingly "critical consciousness" (p. 19) and the "practice of freedom" (p. 15) through a "liberating education" (p. 67).

8. Rich notes that only active reinterpretation of texts will allow women (and other oppressed minorities, I add) to break the hold of oppression (1979, p. 35). Rich calls for "an active transformation of reality" in which individuals begin "to question, to challenge, to conceive of alternatives." As she notes, ". . . nothing can be too sacred for the imagination to turn into its opposite or to call experimentally by another name. For writing is re-naming" (p. 43).

This connection between "naming," revolutionary thinking, and revolution is not exclusive to feminist literature. Freire (1970) notes,

> Human existence cannot be silent, nor can it be nourished by false words, but only by true words, with which men [*sic*] transform the world. To exist, humanly, is to *name* the world, to change it. Once named, the world in its turn reappears to the namers as a problem and requires of them a new *naming*. . . .

. . . dialogue cannot occur between those who want to name the world and those who do not wish this naming—between those who deny other men [sic] the right to speak their word and those whose right to speak has been denied. (p. 76)

9. Although no one source I am familiar with examines all of these inequities, I can suggest several for those readers who want to pursue the study of technological inequity: Becker (February 1987); Chen (1985); and Gomez (1986).

10. As always, much of my thinking in this paper has been informed by my colleagues at Michigan Technological University. In this particular case, Marilyn Cooper and Billie Wahlstrom have helped me wrestle with some of the more difficult conceptual connections I tried to establish in this text, and Ruthan Ruehr, Eunice Carlson, and Elizabeth Flynn provided me with reference materials that were much needed. Who among us exists without connections?

WORKS CITED

Arms, Valarie, ed. *IEEE Transactions on Professional Communications: Special Issue on Computer Conferencing.* PC-29.1 (March 1986).

Batson, Trent. "The ENFI Project: A Networked Classroom Approach to Writing Instruction." *Academic Computing* February/March (1988): 32–33.

Becker, Henry Jay. "Using Computers for Instruction." *BYTE* (February 1987): 149–162.

Bernhardt, Steve, and Bruce Appleby. "Collaboration in Professional Writing with the Computer." *Computers and Composition* 3, no. 1 (1985): 29–42.

Bowen, Betsy, and Jeffrey Schwartz. "What's Next for Computers: Electronic Networks in the Writing Classroom." Paper given at the annual meeting of the National Council of Teachers of English, San Antonio, November 1986.

Catano, James V. "Computer-Based Writing: Navigating the Fluid Text." *College Composition and Communication* 36 (1985): 309–316.

Caywood, Cynthia L., and Gillian R. Overing. *Teaching Writing: Pedagogy, Gender, and Equity.* Albany: State University of New York, 1987.

Chen, Milton. "Gender Differences in Computer Use and Attitudes." Paper given at the thirty-fifth annual conference of the International Communication Association, Honolulu, 1985.

"Computer Talks to Downs Kids." *Milwaukee Journal* (December 14, 1987): D4.

Cooper, Marilyn. "Theory and Practice: The Case of Technical Communication Programs." Unpublished manuscript. Michigan Technological University, Houghton, 1987.

Daiute, Colette. "Issues in Using Computers to Socialize the Writing Process." *ECTJ: Educational Communication and Technology* 33, no. 1 (1985): 41–50.

Däumer, Elisabeth, and Sandra Runzo. "Transforming the Composition Classroom." *Teaching Writing: Pedagogy, Gender, and Equity.* Ed. Cynthia L. Caywood and Gillian R. Overing. Albany: State University of New York, 1987, pp. 45–62.

Eldred, Janet. "Computers, Composition Pedagogy, and the Social View." *Critical Perspectives on Computers and Composition Instruction*. Ed. Gail Hawisher and Cynthia Selfe. New York: Teachers College, 1989, pp. 201–218.

Fersko-Weiss, Henry. "Electronic Mail: The Emerging Connection." *Personal Computing* (January 1985): 71–79.

Firestone, Shulamith. "On American Feminism." *Woman in Sexist Society: Studies in Power and Powerlessness*. Ed. Vivian Gornick and Barbara K. Moran. New York: Basic Books, 1971, pp. 485–501.

Freire, Paulo. *Pedagogy of the Oppressed*. Trans. Myra Bergman Ramos. New York: Seabury Press, 1970.

Frey, Olivia. "Equity and Peace in the New Writing Class." *Teaching Writing: Pedagogy, Gender, and Equity*. Ed. Cynthia L. Caywood and Gillian R. Overing, Albany: State University of New York, 1987, pp. 93–105.

Gilligan, Carol. *In a Different Voice: Psychological Theory and Women's Development*. Cambridge, MA: Harvard, 1982.

Gomez, Mary Louise. "Equity, English, and Computers." *Wisconsin English Journal* 29, no. 1 (1986): 18–22.

Gornick, Vivian. "Woman as Outsider." *Woman in Sexist Society: Studies in Power and Powerlessness*. Ed. Vivian Gornick and Barbara K. Moran. New York: Basic Books, 1971, pp. 70–84.

———, and Barbara K. Moran, eds. *Woman in Sexist Society: Studies in Power and Powerlessness*. New York: Basic Books, 1971.

Hawisher, Gail. "Studies in Word Processing." *Computers and Composition* 4, no. 1 1986: 6–31.

Heim, Michael. *Electric Language: A Philosophical Study of Word Processing*. New Haven, CT: Yale, 1987.

Hiltz, Starr Roxanne. "The 'Virtual Classroom': Using Computer-Mediated Communication for University Teaching." *Journal of Communication* 36, no. 2 (1986): 95–104.

Holmsten, Vicki. "What Is Macy's Anyway? New York Comes to the Indian Reservation via E-Mail." Paper given at the annual meeting of the National Council of Teachers of English, Los Angeles, 1987.

Holvig, Kenneth. "Voices across the Wires through Breadnet and Clarknet." Paper given at the annual meeting of the National Council of Teachers of English, Los Angeles, 1987.

Humphreys, David. "A Computer-Training Program for English Teachers: Cuyahoga Community College and the Urban Initiatives Action Program." *Computers in English and Language Arts: The Challenge of Teacher Education*. Ed. Cynthia Selfe, Dawn Rodrigues, and William Oates, Urbana, IL: National Council of Teachers of English, 1989, pp. 3–16.

Kiesler, Sara, Jane Siegel, and Timothy W. McGuire. "Social Psychological Aspects of Computer-Mediated Communication." *American Psychologist* 39 (1984): 1123–1134.

Lanham, Richard. "Convergent Pressures: Social, Technological, Theoretical." Paper presented at the Conference on the Future of Doctoral Studies in English, Wayzata, MN, April 1987.

Ludtke, Melissa. "Great Human Power or Magic: An Innovative Program Sparks the Writing of America's Children." *Time* (September 14, 1987): 76.

Meek, Brock. "The Quiet Revolution: On-Line Education Becomes a Real Alternative." *BYTE* (February 1987): 183-190.

Meyers, Greg. "Greg Meyers Responds." *College English* 49 (1987): 211-214.

Mielke, Robert. "Revisionist Theory on Moral Development and Its Impact upon Pedagogical and Departmental Practice." *Teaching Writing: Pedagogy, Gender and Equity.* Ed. Cynthia L. Caywood and Gillian R. Overing. Albany: State University of New York, 1987, pp. 171-178.

Miller, Casey, and Swift, Kate. *Words and Women: New Language in New Times.* Garden City, NY: Anchor, 1976.

Nelson, Cary. "Against English: Theory and the Limits of the Discipline." *Profession 87* (1987): 46-52.

Nilsen, Alleen Pace, et al. *Sexism and Language.* Urbana, IL: National Council of Teachers of English, 1977.

Ohmann, Richard, "Literacy, Technology, and Monopoly Capital." *College English* 47 (1985): 675-689.

Olsen, Tillie. *Silences.* New York: Dell, 1986.

Patraka, Vivian. "Notes on Technique in Feminist Drama: Apple Pie and Signs of Life." *Feminist Re-visions: What Has Been and Might Be.* Ed. Vivian Patraka and Louise Tilly. Ann Arbor: The Women's Studies Program of the University of Michigan, 1983, pp. 43-63.

————, and Louise Tilly. *Feminist Re-visions: What Has Been and Might Be.* Ann Arbor: The Women's Studies Program of the University of Michigan, 1983.

Perry, Donna M. "Making Journal Writing Matter." *Teaching Writing: Pedagogy, Gender, and Equity.* Ed. Cynthia L. Caywood and Gillian R. Overing. Albany: State University of New York, 1987, pp. 151-156.

Pfaffenberger, Bryan. "Research Networks, Scientific Communication, and the Personal Computer." *IEEE Transaction on Professional Communication: Special Issue on Computer Conferencing.* Ed. Valarie Arms. PC-29.1 (March 1986): 30-33.

Pullinger, D. J. "Chit-Chat to Electronic Journals: Computer Conferencing Supports Scientific Communication." *IEEE Transaction on Professional Communication: Special Issue on Computer Conferencing.* Ed. Valarie Arms. PC-29.1 (March 1986): 23-29.

Quinn, Mary A. "Teaching Digression as a Mode of Discovery: A Student-Centered Approach to the Discussion of Literature." *Teaching Writing: Pedagogy, Gender, and Equity.* Ed. Cynthia L. Caywood and Gillian R. Overing. Albany: State University of New York, 1987, pp. 123-134.

Rabinowitz, Paula, "Naming, Magic, and Documentary: The Subversion of the Narrative in *Song of Solomon, Ceremony* and *China Men.*" *Feminist Re-visions: What Has Been and Might Be.* Ed. Vivian Patraka and Louise Tilly. Ann Arbor: The Women's Studies Program of the University of Michigan, 1983, pp. 26-42.

Rich, Adrienne. *On Lies, Secrets, and Silence: Selected Prose 1966-78* New York: Norton, 1979.

Reinharz, Shulamit. "Feminist Research Methodology Groups: Origins, Forms, Functions." *Feminist Re-visions: What Has Been and Might Be.* Ed. Vivian Patraka and Louise Tilly. Ann Arbor: The Women's Studies Program of the University of Michigan, 1983, pp. 197–228.

Rodrigues, Dawn. "Computers and Basic Writers." *College Composition and Communication* 36 (1985): 336–339.

Sargent, Pamela, ed. *Women of Wonder: Science Fiction Stories by Women about Women.* New York: Vintage Books, 1974.

Selfe, Cynthia. "Computers in English Departments: The Rhetoric of Technopower." *ADE Bulletin* 90 (1988): 63–67.

———. "Redefining Literacy: The Multi-Layered Grammars of Computers." Paper given at the annual Conference on College Composition and Communication, Atlanta, March 1987.

———. and John Eilola. "The Tie That Binds: Building Group Cohesion through Computer-Based Conferences." *Collegiate Microcomputer* 6, no. 4 (1988): 339–348.

———. and Billie J. Wahlstrom. "Computers and Writing: Casting a Broader Net with Theory and Research." *Computers and the Humanities* 22 (1988): 57–66.

———. and Billie J. Wahlstrom. "Computer-Supported Writing Classes: Lessons for Teachers." *Computers in English and Language Arts: The Challenge of Teacher Education.* Ed. Cynthia Selfe, Dawn Rodrigues, and William Oates. Urbana, IL: National Council of Teachers of English, 1989, pp. 257–268.

———. and Billie J. Wahlstrom. "An Emerging Rhetoric of Collaboration: Computers and the Composing Process." *Collegiate Microcomputer* 4, no. 4 (1985): 289–295.

Spender, Dale. *Man Made Language.* London: Metheun, 1985.

Spitzer, Michael. "Computer Conferencing: An Emerging Technology." *Critical Perspectives on Computers and Composition Instruction.* Ed. Gail Hawisher and Cynthia Selfe. New York: Teachers College, 1989, pp. 187–200.

———. "Writing Style in Computer Conferences." *IEEE Transaction on Professional Communication: Special Issue on Computer Conferencing.* Ed. Valarie Arms. PC-29.1 (1986): 19–22.

Steeves, H. Leslie. "Feminist Theories and Media Studies." *Critical Studies in Mass Communication* 4, no. 2 (1987): 95–135.

Stine, Linda. "Computers and Commuters: Making a Difficult Connection." Paper given at the annual meeting of the National Council of Teachers of English, Los Angeles, 1986.

Techno/Peasant Survival Manual, The. A Print-Project Book. New York: Bantam Books, 1980. Copyright by Colette Dowling.

Wittig, Monique. *Les Guérillères.* New York: Avon Books, 1969.

Zimmerman, Don H., and Candace West. "Sex Roles, Interruptions and Silences in Conversation." *Language and Sex: Difference and Dominance.* Ed. Barrie Thorne and Nancy Henley. Rowley, MA: Newberry House Publishers, 1975, pp. 105–129.

The Social Shifts Invited by Working Collaboratively on Computer Networks: The ENFI Project

M. DIANE LANGSTON
ICL North America

TRENT W. BATSON
Gallaudet University

ENFI (Electronic Networks for Interaction) offers a new channel for communication and collaboration in the writing classroom
that consists of a local-area network bolstered by communication
software that allows a group to "converse" in writing. The use of
this new channel seems to invite shifts in the social interactions of
the classroom. When people communicate in writing, the normal
social hierarchies, communication patterns, and work styles that
exist in a regular classroom are affected. The shifts can be both
disruptive and helpful, and they are only sparsely described so far,
but those who are using ENFI-based methods have been surprised
that a seemingly simple innovation implies so much. Now, a community of researchers is exploring ways to turn the shifts to the
teacher's advantage.

At this writing, about 25 colleges and universities are using
ENFI-based methods in writing classrooms. Not all of the projects
are called "ENFI," but since the ENFI Project at Gallaudet University in Washington, DC, was the first to try such a method of using
computer networks in 1985 and all the other projects are similar
in some sense, the term ENFI can serve as a convenient classifier

for the many network-based approaches in use at different sites. In this chapter, we characterize some of the shifts that ENFI-based methods help create in the writing classroom—from presentational to environmental teaching modes, from a primary teaching role of evaluator to participant/leader, from an instructional strategy geared to recitation to one involving collaboration, from a focus on the individual as the locus of composition to a more social view, and finally, the larger implications for the shift from print to electronic media as the primary technology of communication, in the spirit of Walter Ong, Eric Havelock, and Marshall McLuhan.

INTRODUCTION: A SCENE FROM AN ENFI CLASS

It is Monday morning at 8:45, almost time for your English 101 class. You leave your office and walk down the hall to Room 548, which has 20 personal computers, all networked. (You may or may not have a dedicated server in the room, or be networked through the campus network, depending on your particular networking configuration.) Some of your students are already typing away at their computers, finishing some work for today's class. A few students not enrolled in your class also work at other computers. You sit at the "teacher station," which is like the other computers in the room except that you have a few more controls. Behind your computer is a large whiteboard, a vestige of the traditional classroom you have relinquished.

At 8:55, you ask the students working in the room who are not registered for your class to leave because your class is about to begin. By nine, most of your own students are present and logged onto the network. They have learned the routine and realize they need to arrive a few minutes early to be able to participate in the class right from the start.

You hand back floppy disks that some students gave you on Friday containing their dialogue journal entries for the week and tell the others that you have replied to their entries sent to you via e-mail. Still addressing the class orally, you make some comments about the work for this week. Only about a third of the students look at you; the others look at their screens. A couple are walking around getting or offering help with logging in.

You move back to your station, sit down, and engage in some opening online banter with the students.

YOU: I see you're all bright-eyed and bushy-tailed this morning.

CAROL: Groan.

BILL: You must be joking.

YOU: You know I never joke.

WILLIAM: Where's the Duke this morning?

YOU: I think weekends should be outlawed.

MAGIN: Where did that saying come from? Bright-eyed, etc.?

WANDA: I think he's still in NY.

CAROL: Outlaw weekends?

DAVID: I'm not bright-eyed, I know that.

BILL: Do you have my journal, Teach?

YOU: Weekends make it hard for us serious teachers who want to see our students suffer under an unbearable load of work so they'll become brilliant. (Yes, Bill, I have your journal; don't know where Duke is, William; not sure, Magin.)

CAROL: Double groan.

And so on . . .

After five minutes, you announce that you will demonstrate "freewriting" while the students watch on their screens. You flip a switch that allows all the students to watch your screen (and also prevents them from seeing on their screens whatever they might type). You also switch out of the "chat" program—the one that allows you all to have an online "conversation"—and into a word-processing program (accomplished by hitting a two-key sequence). Then, while the class watches, you demonstrate your personal style of freewriting to find a topic. This takes five minutes. You then stand and comment orally to the class about what they have just seen. You answer a few questions about freewriting.

Next, you announce that the class will divide into four groups of five, each group freewriting together on the network. (The software allows for different groups to have their own "channels" and thereby work independently of each other.) They must agree on a topic within their group in 10 minutes.

The four groups move to their own channels and start work, communicating almost entirely on-line. You hear only the sound of keys clicking after they get going, interspersed with occasional laughter and some side comments. One of the students raises his hand and asks if his group has to agree on a topic. You confirm that they do. "Really?" he asks. Another student has a technical problem and one of the more experienced students in class helps out. You stay at your station, switching your display from one group to another, monitoring their progress. You interject an occasional comment on their screens. The students all work using the "chat" program, so they are working in a dialogue environment, more conversational than compositional. They are working in a shared workspace.

After 10 minutes, you ask the groups if they have agreed on a topic. Most say they are nearly finished. Once they finish, each group gets a printout of their group discussion. You discuss orally with the class how individual freewriting is different from group freewriting—the individual kind serving either as a way of getting started or a means of remembering relevant information, the group kind more an exercise in negotiation to agree on one topic. Next you demonstrate brainstorming as you did freewriting. As the class continues that day, they keep shifting from demonstration on-line to practice on-line to oral discussion and back to demonstration. The students use the printouts from these sessions to help in writing their individual out-of-class papers.

On other days, you might be more directly involved in an online working session with a group of, say, 10 students while the other 10 work independently. Because you now have the ability to display emerging text and to comment during its production, many new options are open to you. The example class described in brief here is only one of many possibilities. The teacher in an ENFI class can work in many new ways, limited only by the amount of experimentation he or she is willing to attempt. ENFI has been used with underprepared students and with very capable ones, with remedial classes and with upper-level classes such as writing for the professions, drama, poetry, editing, and others. In each case, new pedagogical approaches have been possible and, we believe, the social nature of the class has been affected.

FROM PRESENTATIONAL TO ENVIRONMENTAL

When a teacher moves from a regular classroom to an ENFI-based approach using a computer network, the practical means of working are altered, but more profound shifts also take place. For example, the social roles of both teacher and students seem to be affected regardless of whether the teacher intends such a change. By enabling students to take a more active part in the class, ENFI favors the use of approaches that are, in George Hillocks' terms, more "environmental" than "presentational." According to Hillocks, the presentational mode

> is characterized by (1) relatively clear and specific objectives, e.g., to use particular rhetorical techniques; (2) lecture and teacher-led discussion dealing with concepts to be learned and applied; (3) the study of models and other materials which explain and illustrate the concept; (4) specific assignments or exercises which generally involve imitating a pattern or following rules that have been previously discussed; and (5) feedback following the writing, coming primarily from teachers. (1986, p. 117)

By contrast, the environmental mode

> is characterized by (1) clear and specific objectives, e.g., to increase the use of specific detail and figurative language; (2) materials and problems selected to engage students with each other in specifiable processes important to some particular aspect of writing; and (3) activities, such as small-group problem-centered discussions, conducive to high levels of peer interaction concerning specific tasks. (p. 122)

Although students take a stronger role when environmental approaches are used, Hillocks stresses that teachers in both environmental and presentational modes still develop and work toward clear and specific learning objectives.[1] The main difference between the two modes is that in the presentational mode the teacher remains the focus or initiator of activities, whereas in the environmental mode the peer group working within the limits of the tasks set by the teacher is more the focus. The teacher moves away from directing both the overall goals of the class and how students work toward those goals, and places more responsibility on the students to choose and pursue their own means of attaining the course goals. Studies of learning suggest that the more engaged a person is in learning, the more likely it is that learning will take place (for example, Laffey 1982; Osborne and Wittrock 1983).

Hillocks considers a shift from presentational to environmental modes to be a positive change; using the computer network appears to facilitate classroom methods that are more environmental. For example, environmental modes involve a social context for writing. In a regular classroom, writing teachers sometimes attempt to create social contexts by providing assignments such as case-based tasks that provide a full rhetorical situation or involve a real-life purpose, like complaining to a company about a faulty product or service. However, case-based assignments can seem artificial and, as Knoblauch and Brannon (1984) observe, can require students to work in domains with which they are not familiar enough to develop strong responses to the task. Similarly, writing for so-called real-life purposes often involves contexts that are too trivial to be interesting, since opportunities for students to have a substantial impact via writing on the problems they consider to be most important are often limited. In addition, a traditional classroom often does not provide significant occasions for students to interact with each other and establish a social context in that way. Peer-group work takes place in a face-to-face setting, where the social hierarchy of the classroom may be retained regardless of a teacher's efforts to create an informal, collegial atmosphere. Those students who dominate classroom discussions are also likely to dominate small-group discussions, despite attempts to draw in reticent ones or those whose learning style results in a more deliberate interactive style (Gardner 1983), defeating the social purposes of group work.

In computer-based working groups, on the other hand, social roles become more blurred (Sproull and Kiesler 1986; Sirc 1988; Kremers 1988). Participants who don't generally dominate face-to-face interactions are likely to speak more strongly when communicating on-line (Mabrito 1989). In a pilot study at Carnegie Mellon University in 1988, we found indications that groups working on-line will show a more evenly distributed interactive pattern than face-to-face groups. Two students in a group of four working together on a collaborative paper dominated the face-to-face discussion, the most active one taking 33 percent of all conversational turns while one of the less active took only 7 percent of the turns, most of which were brief interjections. A similar group in the same class working on-line divided turns evenly, each taking about 25 percent of the total turns (Batson and Langston 1988). Another study suggests that women and minorities enjoy a more active role on-line than face to face (Bump 1989). Other studies reported at the 1989 Conference on College Composition and Communication both contradicted and supported this finding, suggesting that further research is necessary before the "democratizing" effects of computer-based classroom interaction are fully understood.

Teachers often worry that with ENFI-based methods, the fastest typist will dominate the online conversation just as the fastest or boldest talker does in face-to-face interaction; however, that situation does not generally occur. On the network, several students can type at once, making it harder for one to shut out the others as they can in face-to-face meetings where exchanges take place sequentially. In addition, one's voice is closer to "home" psychologically than is one's written message; many emotional associations and sanctions are linked to vocal expression ("Children are meant to be seen, not heard"; "If you can't say something nice, don't say anything at all"; "If you don't stop crying, I'll give you something to really cry about"; and so on). Written expression, since it is learned later than speech and is less intimately tied to an individual speaker, may be a less emotionally charged communication channel. Such tendencies—toward more even turn taking, increased minority participation, and less inhibition in interacting—help explain why ENFI-based classrooms lend themselves to teaching approaches that are more environmental.

FROM EVALUATOR TO PARTICIPANT/LEADER

Surveys of students indicate that a large percentage of under-graduates believe the sole purpose of writing is to get a grade (Fulwiler 1987). School-based writing is inevitably associated with evaluation, which can undercut student engagement by making writing seem more like a demanded performance than like a search for personally relevant meanings (cf. Knoblauch and Brannon 1984, p. 108). Suppose, for example, that every time a student talked in class, he or she was audiotaped and graded on the utterance for correctness, cogency, and coherence. Discussion could be considerably stifled. However, in the classroom, talking is not usually part of the evaluation process except in terms of class participation. The number of turns taken is often as important as the quality of the utterances. Once pen is put to paper, though, evaluation begins in earnest, and under that condition, students often provide a jumble of words and phrases—what Ken Macrorie (1970) has called "Engfish"—in an effort to provide what they believe the teacher wants.

The "Engfish" phenomenon leaves writing teachers in a difficult situation. On the one hand, teachers want to set specific learning goals, maintain standards, and strive toward a certain model of good writing; on the other, teachers suspect that unless students are fully engaged in the writing task and can personalize it to some extent for themselves, they will never reach those learning goals. One way of resolving the conflict is to spend more class time on the early phases of writing, the moments in which critical decisions are being made about everything from subject matter to perspective, that can improve or discourage engage-ment. However, a difficulty arises: In a paper-based classroom, it is hard to intervene in the early moments of writing, even if class time is devoted to them. Teachers cannot really watch over the students' shoulders and comment on emerging ideas and text; there are too many students, and early drafting with pen and paper takes too much time.

In the ENFI-based classroom, however, with students and teachers writing to each other on a local-area network, the teacher can take a more active coaching role in the early moments of composing. The teacher can either join large groups of, say, 10 students and engage in collaborative inventional work with them or observe and assist from her workstation as several smaller groups work together. The teacher can also participate more actively in revision with a network, modeling revision activities and strategies that students can adopt for their own work. As a genuine partner in the process of text creation and revision, the teacher can begin to move away from a stultifying one-dimensional role as evaluator in the classroom.

FROM RECITATION TO COLLABORATION

Many composition teachers feel uncomfortable with the artificiality of the rhetorical situation created for students in writing classes. Students are asked to write about subjects they often know little about, yet they must write with authority. They may not care at all about the subject but are expected to be enthusiastic; though really writing for a grade, they are expected to be personally involved. They are unfamiliar with the academic tone they are expected to adopt and also with the imaginary audience they are supposed to address. Much of their writing takes on the air of "recitation," rote performance rather than active engagement.

However, like teachers, students have new options in ENFI-based classes. Creating the first draft of a paper by working conversationally on a computer network allows groups to alternate between commenting on the process and generating text to keep. The distinction between talk—a relatively unevaluated component of class—and writing—the most evaluated component—becomes blurred. The result is that often the students carry forward into their writing some of the energy and fluency that characterizes their talk.

In addition, the network makes small-group collaboration straightforward and keeps separate records of the work each group accomplishes, available in a printout at the end of class.[2] Small-group work on ENFI affords students the opportunity to write to a real and present audience. Studies suggest that some kinds of writers—basic writers particularly—write better when they write directly to another person than when responding to assigned writing tasks (Cummins 1981; Heath and Branscombe 1985). Phrases that such writers use comfortably when writing to a friend may be produced incorrectly or disappear altogether from their writing in class and their overall competence suffers. Even for the better writer, who may have internalized a sense of audience, immediate feedback still provides valuable information, whether from fellow students or the teacher.

Small-group work can take many forms on the network. For example, a technique used at Carnegie-Mellon involved pairs of students rather than groups of three or four. The two students sat at separate workstations on the network and read each other's working draft only a few lines at a time. After reviewing each short section, the reader's task was to write what he or she thought the writer should say next. This technique encouraged both students to focus on the development of the essay as it progressed, rather than on the whole essay, which is often too large a unit for freshmen to comment on in detail.

Online commenting via the network can also provide an immediacy of response that students seldom receive otherwise, bringing the social context of writing even closer. If the writer is on-line at the same time as a commenting partner, a dialogue can ensue with revisions being made and tested against the partner immediately. Online comments can more easily point to specific parts of the student's text—via insertions in a text editor or special commenting programs—and provide more specific information than the general summary comment that members of peer working groups often provide in a traditional classroom. In addition, students may make more extensive and honest comments on-line (Kremers 1988).

The opportunity for distance interaction between ENFI-based classes extends the social dimensions of writing even further. At Northern Virginia Community College, for example, students on two separate campuses work together through the network, developing their entire relationship through writing. Students start out in a large general group, say 45 students working in groups of 4, all sharing one computer station. About 11 stations on 2 campuses are involved, and the teachers also participate. Teachers begin discussion of a topic; as the topic gains interest for the groups, they switch the groups out into separate channels so that one group of four on campus A is linked to one group of four on campus B. Eventually, each group breaks contact with the other campus but continues to work together around their one computer.

ENFI-based classes can provide opportunities for writing to become the medium of lively exchange, not merely the self-conscious performance that many students associate with writing for a grade. To the extent that such online exchanges find their way into the drafting process, writing ceases to be so recitative and becomes more social and collaborative.

FROM INDIVIDUAL TO SOCIAL

Increasingly, teachers and theorists are becoming interested in the social aspects of composing (Bruffee 1986; Faigley 1986; LeFevre 1987). Viewed from a social perspective, writing is the product of a constant dialectic between individuals and the society around them. Discourse does not originate as an isolated event in the mind of the writer, but develops in response to "a constant potentiality that is occasionally evidenced in speech or writing. The beginnings and ends of rhetorical acts are thus not clearly obvious or absolute" (Lefevre 1987).

An interesting example of this process appears in a recent book called *Digging Dinosaurs* by John R. Horner and James Gorman. Horner at several times makes explicit the imagined dialogue that surrounded his work and the writing of his book.

> Another way of interpreting fossils is to use the indirect evidence of the environment, the geological evidence on both the large and the small scale. Often concentrations of fossil bone are deceptive [he is now setting up one possible objection to his line of reasoning]; one can be fooled into thinking that the animals found together in death were also together in life, when, for example, what really happened was that they all died near the same stream at different times and were carried by the flow of water to the same spot. In the case of these [dinosaur] babies, however, I don't think we were fooled [answering an imagined critic]. Remember, they were found in a bowl of

green mudstone that was set off by a sharply defined boundary from the surrounding red mudstone. (1988, p. 58)

Although Horner does not provide the identity of his interlocutor(s), he anticipates and answers the kinds of critical questions that his discipline asks of new work in the field. Although his act of individual creativity (the book) has his name on it, he seems aware that he is primarily transforming and adding to an ongoing dialectic within his peer group of paleontologists. According to the basic premises of the social approaches to writing—for example, that invention is an act initiated by writers and completed by readers and that the self that invents is itself socially constructed— then inventional acts may be more individualistic than others, but none is purely the work of an individual.

In a paper-and-print environment, it is difficult to view invention from a social perspective; indeed, the notion of the individual apparently developed concurrently with the dissemination of writing as a technology in ancient Greece (Havelock 1963; Ong 1982). The existence of a paper document implies that it is the artifact of the one person or, at best, two people whose names appear at its beginning. Its status as a self-contained unit that can be exchanged and annotated in the margins supports the belief that all the thoughts and words on the paper came originally from the head of the author, when in fact he or she may have contributed only a unique ordering to existing ideas.

However, in an electronic, conversational writing environment, the position of individuals in ongoing social dialectics is more obvious and concrete. The stream of dialectic is palpable and capturable (as a printout of the conversation), and the notion of any one person "owning" the conversation as it flows by on the screen seems less appropriate, even though individuals make important contributions to the development of the ideas. Collaboration and social context attain a practical reality.

In addition, writing is less fragmented on-line than in more traditional classrooms, where students may discuss a topic in class and then, much later, individually write about and develop ideas from their conversations. Instead of separating in time and space the discussion and the composition that arises from it, conversation and text are merged in an ENFI-based classroom, highlighting the social processes that underlie composition. Students' work on the network can be aimed less at producing writing that the teacher supposedly "wants" and more at negotiating meaning among colleagues, an activity more closely related to the skills that job-related writing often requires.

The limitations of paper and print for encouraging both the spirit and the skills of negotiating meaning are clear. Paper is difficult to share; only one person can write on standard-size paper at a time. In some ways, paper and print support presentational modes of instruction; paper enables one person to take notes easily on the presentation of another (the teacher), but collaborative work is often limited to tiny marginal comments on completed texts that are difficult both to read and to write.

FROM PRINT TO ELECTRONIC MEDIA

In the simplest sense, the shift from a print-based writing classroom to an electronic one has been the subject of this entire book. In another sense, however, the shift from print as a technology of communication to electronic media has profound implications for how our society creates, preserves, and manipulates knowledge— implications that go far beyond how to hook up computers and use them productively in today's writing classes. As these larger shifts occur, the role and task of writers in society can be expected to change; consequently, the focus of instruction in writing classes is likely to change as well. ENFI-based classes seem uniquely situated to adapt to changing conceptions of writing and writers. In this last section, we consider four of the many possible changes that electronic media may bring and how ENFI fits with them.

First, the metaphors by which society understands and speaks of what writers do are likely to change. In classical Greece, the writer was a knowledge seeker. Eric Havelock (1963) associates the widespread use of writing with the cultural changes that Plato helped to establish; among those was the realization that knowledge was separate from the knower, something that individuals could seek or discover and accumulate over the years. In the age of print, perhaps the primary metaphor for writing has been the act of expression, in which ideas inside the writer are expressed or pushed out so that others can see them. Walter Ong suggests that print culture gave rise to the romantic notion of originality, which provides a way for one individual work or text to be set apart from others (1982, p. 133), as well as supporting the movement toward empirical science, which treats knowledge as essentially removed from human interpretation.

In the era of electronic media, new metaphors for writing are needed. One that seems particularly apt is to view the writer as a precipitating solid in a supersaturated solution, essentially the speck of dust around which crystals form. The individual is suspended in the ideas and concepts of society and culture, where her qualities and interests can form the seed for the crystallization of ideas and texts. Composition in the interconnected world of electronic media may be less an act of expression (out of the mind onto paper) than of compression or magnetism, drawing ideas together in unique constellations (an anti-entropic or organizing activity). Metaphors are important; as George Lakoff and Mark Johnson (1980) suggest, they are capable of changing our conception of and approaches to the activities to which they refer. A change to the metaphor by which writing is represented could have implications for the creation of knowledge in many disciplines.

A second and related change involves the writer's goal in the face of the proliferation of information and views about that information that electronic media make available. Although the impetus toward providing new or original information that characterized the role of writers during the print era will doubtless continue, a new impetus focused on creating coherence may arise with the multiplicity of electronic texts. The writer's role may increasingly include the development of perspectives through which masses of data can be productively viewed, providing coherence for what can otherwise be a jumble of events, opinions, biases, and interrelationships. In addition, new demands may be placed on the articulation of points of view; whereas it has traditionally been sufficient simply to state the benefits of a new perspective in its own terms, respect for multiple perspectives may become increasingly important as electronic media make more ideas and opinions available. Finally, since no one individual can expect to master such a flood of information in a lifetime, the importance of recitation and mastery may diminish, giving way to new skills of synthesis and evaluation.

Third, the electronic representations of various kinds of data are converging, making the resources of film, graphics, spreadsheets, and digitized pictures available to writers. Along with the opportunity comes the expectation that writers will master such resources and use them. In technical writing, for example, manuals that are primarily text are no longer acceptable.

However, with this change comes an unexpected effect: The new media bring with them emotional elements that writers did not have to deal with before. For example, an interactive videodisk program developed by Preston Covey, Scott Roberts, and Robert Cavalier (1988) at Carnegie Mellon University focuses on the ethics of allowing a patient to die. In this program, "A Right to Die," interviews with a young man who has been horribly burned and who lives in constant pain relieved occasionally by immersion into an anti-infection fluid and who therefore wants to die are supplemented with interviews with parents, doctors, nurses, and others who are directly involved in the case. As the program progresses, there are pause points when students are asked to reflect and enter responses about what they have seen so far. During those pauses, the lifelike image of the most recent interviewee remains on the screen, "watching" the student as she attempts to decide what should be the fate of the young man. The program resumes once the student has finished entering her response but does not simply follow a linear path. Depending on how the student has responded, the program will choose a path designed to show interviews with involved people who supply ideas or positions that will lead the student in new directions. In this way, ethics is no longer merely theoretical. Programs like this one suggest the ways in which pictures and video may make text more emotionally demanding for both readers and writers. More is at stake than simply mastering new technological opportunities; increasingly the writer must deal with the feelings that come with real-life events that are brought in compellingly realistic form directly to the writer's workplace. She sees and hears the events rather than just reading about them.

Fourth, information is increasingly expected to cross disciplinary boundaries. At first glance, computers appear to be fragmenting knowledge; the flood of information they make available requires that individuals master a relatively narrow part of their respective disciplines in order to be able to sort and evaluate the new findings that arrive at an ever-increasing pace. In the age of computers, it seems possible to look into ever-smaller minutiae, to shrink our view to smaller and smaller phenomena. However, at a certain level of particularity, we may paradoxically find a new opportunity for recombination. For example, perhaps only after knowledge about the natural cycles of the earth reached a sufficiently detailed level was the development of ecology finally possible, representing an effort that crosses disciplinary boundaries to understand the interrelationships among (at least) the social, technological, and organic factors that affect how the earth operates.

To take another example, consider the researcher in a library, looking through the index of a book. The grain of an index is determined by the indexer, not by the reader, and is often quite coarse, referring to entire sections of the book by single labels. The same researcher in an online search has the capacity to search electronic indexes built around key words that are often more extensive and often can do "free-text" searches that involve every single word in a given work. Hence, a single search of an electronic database on particular key words might retrieve articles from a variety of disciplines. The researcher is then free to decide for herself which elements of a work in another field may be relevant to her own work. Because the fragments of knowledge have become so small—down in this case to the individual words of a text—knowledge across disciplines is more accessible than ever. Perhaps we are presented with new means of creating combinations, a new conception of research, and new expectations of the creative writer.

How does ENFI fit with our discussion so far of the shift from print to electronic media? First, ENFI helps people move beyond a notion of the individual creator to the supersaturated analogy. The skill is how to be an effective speck—how to develop habits of mind and inquiry that enable information to "stick" in meaningful ways. Approaches to texts and information that favor "stickiness" can be modeled on-line, as ENFI is particularly well suited to modeling, unlike the regular classroom. In a face-to-face discussion, the teacher may at some point have an aha! experience of seeing new connections among the many made in the oral discussion. Because the teacher is normally the focal point of a face-to-face discussion, however, only she is likely to have the aha! experience, or at least will be the only one to give voice to it. In an online conversation, however, where it is easier for all participants to feel they have more initiative, they are invited themselves to generate their own aha! comments, pointing to connections they have seen among the strands of conversation going ahead. There is a chance to see the contributions of different people contiguously on the screen for a few moments, reflect on them, or even follow a separate subconversation while others are still interacting. Participants have different kinds of opportunities on-line to make connections that they don't have face to face.

Second, ENFI-based experiences allow for multiple perspectives in a controlled setting, enabling students to practice some of the integration and negotiation skills they are likely to need. Other students bring information and perspectives and meaning is negotiated. In ENFI classrooms, the teacher must be able to do more than introduce the topic; she must guide the students toward coherence as well. She can no longer adopt the convenient delusion that all listeners have in their consciousness the same idea-order she has. Instead, she might admit that, like her, the listeners mentally wander around the idea like prowling wolves. The same person conducting an online written conversation will find that the prowlings of the group are no longer invisible and therefore are not so easily ignored but instead immediately evident in the seemingly chaotic computerized display of multiple and disparate written contributions. She is experiencing on a small scale the nightmare of mental transparency: It is as if many of the thoughts in one social context were present at once.

Third, to add to the profusion, one could incorporate access to multimedia data such as the Robert Cavalier program, charts, graphs or other related information, in addition to the multiple voices available on ENFI. Many products for using multimedia can be used over a network; it is easy to imagine their use alongside an ENFI-based conversational system. A conversational system could also provide an appropriate frame for text-generating programs in a future computerized environment.

Fourth, the fluidity of online work also makes it easier to engage in "boundary hopping," where knowledge from many disciplines is imported directly into the classroom while discussion is proceeding. Compact disk–based programs like "A Right to Die" may make it more straightforward to have the subject matter of disciplines be the subject matter for writing on a small enough scale so that students can more easily see how one set of concerns raises or addresses similar issues in another field. In addition, the possibility for distance hookups means that subject matter experts can "sit in on" the class from their office and answer questions or provide perspectives that help students see across disciplinary boundaries.

Hence, ENFI can be used in ways that form an introduction to new ways of knowing that computers may bring. It is more than a device for teaching writing better; it has the potential to be a window or a vehicle to the future. In the best sense of education, students using ENFI can encounter some of the new informational principles of the interconnected age.

NOTES

1. The other two modes that Hillocks discusses, natural process and individual, are not generally built around specific learning objectives but are oriented to finding and addressing specific needs that individual students have.

2. It is possible to achieve computer-based collaboration in the writing classroom without using a network, by having a small group share one screen and pass the keyboard around. The computer display makes the text a shared one because it is visible to all, in the handwriting of none, and not composed on any one person's paper. The words on the screen seem to have a social presence unlike those created by the hand of an individual. However, without the network, such ac-

tivities are available to only three or four students per station, and the best typist among them may do most of the text generating.

WORKS CITED

Batson, Trent, and M. Diane Langston. "Two Recent Cognitive Studies of ENFI-Based Instruction: Results and Implications." Paper given at the Computers in Writing and Language Instruction Conference, Duluth, MN, August 1–2, 1988.

Bruffee, Kenneth A. "Social Construction, Language, and the Authority of Knowledge: A Bibliographical Essay." *College English* 48 (1986): 773–790.

Bump, Jerome. "Radical Changes in Class Discussion Using Networked Computers." Paper given at the Conference on College Composition and Communication, Seattle, March 15–18, 1989.

Cavalier, Robert. "Video Discs in Ethics and Aesthetics." Paper given at the Computers in Writing and Language Instruction Conference, Duluth, MN, August 1–2, 1988.

Cummins, James. "The Role of Primary Language Development in Promoting Educational Success for Language Minority Students." *Schooling and Language Minority Students: A Theoretical Framework*. Los Angeles: Evaluation, Dissemination, and Assessment Center, 1981.

Faigley, Lester. "Competing Theories of Process: A Critique and a Proposal." *College English* 48 (1986): 527–542.

Fulwiler, Toby. "Writing across the Curriculum." Workshop presented at the NCTE Winter Workshop, Clearwater, FL, January 5–7, 1987.

Gardner, Howard. *Frames of Mind: The Theory of Multiple Intelligences*. New York: Basic Books, 1983.

Havelock, Eric A. *Preface to Plato*. Cambridge, MA: Belknap–Harvard, 1963.

Heath, Shirley Brice, and Amanda Branscombe. "'Intelligent Writing' in an Audience Community: Teacher, Students, and Researcher." *The Acquisition of Written Language: Response and Revision*. Ed. Sarah Warshauer Freedman. Norwood, NJ: Ablex, 1985, pp. 3–32.

Hillocks, George, Jr. *Research on Written Composition: New Directions for Teaching*. Urbana, IL: ERIC Clearinghouse on Reading and Communication Skills and National Conference on Research in English, 1986.

Horner, John R., and James Gorman. *Digging Dinosaurs*. New York: Workman, 1988.

Knoblauch, C. H., and Lil Brannon. *Rhetorical Traditions and the Teaching of Writing*. Portsmouth, NH: Boynton/Cook, 1984.

Kremers, Marshall. "Adams Sherman Hill Meets ENFI: An Inquiry and a Retrospective." *Computers and Composition* 5, no. 3 (1988): 69–77.

Laffey, James M. "The Assessment of Involvement with School Work among Urban High School Students." *Journal of Educational Psychology* 74 (1982): 62–71.

Lakoff, George, and Mark Johnson. *Metaphors We Live By*. Chicago: University of Chicago, 1980.

LeFevre, Karen Burke. *Invention as a Social Act*. Published for the Conference on College Composition and Communication. Carbondale: Southern Illinois, 1987.

Mabrito, Mark. "Writing Apprehension and Computer-Mediated Writing Groups: A Case Study of the Peer-Evaluation Processes of Four High- and Four Low-Apprehension Writers Face-to-Face versus Electronic Mail." Unpublished dissertation, University of Illinois at Chicago, 1989.

Macrorie, Ken. *Telling Writing*. Rochelle Park, NJ: Hayden, 1970.

Ong, Walter J. *Orality and Literacy: The Technologizing of the Word*. London: Methuen, 1982.

Osborne, R. J., and M. C. Wittrock. "Learning Science: A Generative Process." *Science Education* 67 (1983): 489–508.

Sirc, Geoffrey. "Learning to Write on a LAN." *T.H.E. Journal* 15, no. 8 (April 1988): 99–104.

Sproull, Lee, and Sara Kiesler. "Reducing Social Context Cues: Electronic Mail in Organizational Communication." *Management Science* 32, no. 11 (1986): 1492–1512.

Politics, Ideology, and the Strange, Slow Death of the Isolated Composer or Why We Need Community in the Writing Classroom

CAROLYN HANDA
University of California, Davis

HOW NAIVE
TO BELIEVE
THAT COLLABORATION IN CLASS
HAD ACTUALLY COME TO PASS.

Writing teachers, specifically those in computer classrooms, need to build collaborative techniques consciously into their pedagogies to draw students away from the ideologically specific, isolated approach to writing that word processors too often reinforce. My argument may seem redundant, even unnecessary, given this book's preceding chapters. So before I begin defending this position, I want to take a brief detour.

Some time ago at a conference I sketched out a few ideas for this chapter. Immediately after my presentation I realized my naiveté: I had assumed that the collaborative classroom is now an accepted pedagogical strategy for composition teachers. Collab-

I am grateful to John Boe, Cynthia Bates, and Marlene Clarke for being supportive colleagues and helping me try to refine this chapter's infelicities. I appreciate, especially, the questions Marlene raised as she read my drafts. Many of them I have yet to answer. But answering them will be, as the saying goes, another story.

oration, however, appears a much more controversial topic than I had anticipated. Besides clear, outright rejection, resistance to collaboration takes subtle forms, some that the resistors may not even recognize as such. At the conference, I followed a colleague who spoke eloquently and reasonably against collaboration. In the discussion following our panel, some participants expressed surprise that any instructor in this day and age could defend what they considered an outmoded, authoritative, teacher-centered classroom, but many who spoke out in favor of collaboration betrayed just as much indirect mistrust of the collaborative process as my colleague had expressed openly. A few confessed that they saw themselves as benevolent dictators. Others stressed that as teachers we still need to assert a position as the expert in the class because, "after all, students do give each other bad advice" and "we have been writing a lot longer than they have." These instructors were clearly torn between the two positions. And panelists and audience alike asked, "How crucial is this disagreement for the computer classroom?"

In the following pages I want to clarify what I mean by collaboration, then try to explain (1) why we have such disparate views and (2) what this disparity implies for the teacher in the computer classroom, for an instructor in a computer lab, or for an administrator considering installing a computer classroom or lab. Finally, I want to argue that the computer is not simply neutral. Emerging at a particular period in time, in a particular social context, the computer is a tool reflecting the politics and ideology of both. Clearly, then, those of us using computers to teach composition in our classrooms, more so than in standard composition classrooms, must be aware of these implications and must recognize that we may hide within ourselves a deeply embedded, unconscious resistance to collaboration when we thought we actually favored it. End of detour.

For me, the word *collaboration* covers various levels of activity we consciously undertake during the invention and composing phases of writing and subconsciously draw on during that same time. Collaboration can range from a simple yet active dialogue between a writer and someone she wants reactions from (for example, a colleague or editor) to a complex interchange between one writer and a group she presents her work to for reactions and suggestions. Whatever the degree of complexity, though, collaboration involves a move outward from the writer to others who provide response and input. It is a move away from solipcism.

A writer most keenly aware of the importance of collaboration recognizes that she becomes more creative and intellectually precise when she actively engages in a dialectic with others over her writing. Some of the dialectic may be actual communication with people physically present in the room. Some of it may be less interactive, but it remains communication, nonetheless, with people either living or dead through their ideas in books. Some of it may amount to drawing from what she already knows about her world and those who live in it. We are always collaborating with our environment—our community, that is, and its prevailing cultural attitudes—whether we realize it or not.

Collaboration, then, means much more than just organizing students in groups while we secretly hope they don't "give each other wrong information." It involves getting students to realize consciously how much others—sometimes even those we haven't met—help develop our ideas. Anyone who has ever ransacked the library for information, footnoted another author's text, or incorporated the suggestions of colleagues and editors has collaborated. Collaboration is a spirit that makes an author eager to talk over his work with others, makes him distrust his own work for the blindness he knows it contains. It is actually a spirit that most of us as writers and teachers already possess. But it is something we must work hard to pass on to our students, especially when we, our curriculum, and the machinery we're using sometimes work, unbeknown to us, toward opposite pedagogical ends.

Well over a decade ago, Richard Ohmann (1976) explained in detail how much of a political time and place our pedagogies are, and his "radical views" may—to some extent and to some instructors—still be considered radical today. Ohmann said, "The way we present composition to students has something important to do with how America does politics and makes decisions" (p. 135). He explained the subterranean links he found between the values and folkways of freshman English and America's

military-industrial complex, claiming that "the leaders of indus-
trial society let English teachers know—indirectly, to be sure—what
kind of writing they want; and English teachers help teach the next
generation of leaders what kind of writing to want" (p. 94).

Not only does the way we present composition to students have
something to do with American politics, so does the computer.
The electronic digital computer was, says Richard Lanham (1989),
"a child of war":

> In the computer's case, it was World War II, and the generators of its
> mythology were two. In England, a pioneer calculating machine—
> one whose details are still not publicly known—formed the center of
> the spectacularly successful British code-breaking activities at
> Bletchley Park. In America, the Aberdeen Proving Ground's need for
> a quicker method of calculating artillery trajectories led the Ballis-
> tics Research Laboratory to fund ENIAC, the 18,000-tubed wonder
> which begot the American main-frame computer industry. (p. 1)

Lanham explains how elements of the computer's early history
merged into a type of Platonic mythology containing a "logical
problem-solving AI (Artificial Intelligence) model for thought
which we are only beginning to outgrow" (p. 2). And although "the
electronic Platonism of this mythology still governs, for many
people, the much-changed world of the personal computer," Lanham argues that "this new world is not Platonic at all. . . . It is in
fact a political rather than an oracular world, and the personal
computer as we have socialized it is not . . . finally a numerical
Platonic device but a rhetorical one" (pp. 2–3).

Ohmann's and Lanham's arguments taken together help il-
luminate the behavior we find in our computer composition classrooms today. Our pedagogies imply to students how we think they
receive knowledge, how we think they should try to pass it on. We
may think of our society as running along authoritarian lines and
of knowledge as a neat and tidy equation that one generation can
package and distribute to the next, as something, in other words,
passed down from an oracle, instead of constructed—with the help
of those around us and from the culture surrounding us—for
specific rhetorical situations. If so, our classrooms may well suggest to students that cooperation with others, working with others,
is acceptable only during an informal discussion, but that when we

write seriously, think seriously, and use technology, we learn from an authority. In addition, we only write and think creatively by sitting alone at our terminals. Under such circumstances, the computer comes to resemble that other bugaboo of electronic media, the television, and thus we encourage social behavior around the computer that markedly resembles the "social" behavior or interaction we find around a TV: namely, none.

Today we can still clearly trace a connection between freshman English and the military-industrial complex. In his book, Ohmann highlights a depressing parallel between the writing and thinking of policy theorists and many of the tenets for "good" writing and argumentation propounded by then-current composition textbooks. No great change has taken place in the more than dozen years occurring between his book and this one. Ohmann showed how rarely any policy maker described "his personal involvement, what he has at stake, who he takes to be on his side and who on the other side—much less his social class, family connections, income, race, or sex." Then comes his real blow:

> This same abstraction of circumstances can be found . . . in what the freshman textbooks say about argument, as it is implicit in the way they place the student writer outside history and apart from such categories as wealth, power, and class. . . . Both the advice of the texts and the practice of the theorists and policy-makers are best suited— not only to a technological society that sets great emphasis on expertise, knowledge, and planning—but to those members of such a society with most power and privilege. For this is a rhetoric that masks power and privilege, and any asymmetrical relationships of the writer to his fellow human beings, just as it either masks conflict or suggests that conflict derives from misunderstandings rather than from (say) the resentment of the powerless and their wish to share more equality. (pp. 189–190)

Ohmann's charge that English 101 has helped "to teach the rhetoric of the bureaucrats and technicians" (p. 205) still holds in some part today, depressing though it may be to admit.

> Though the writers of the textbooks and the planners of courses may be generalists and humanists by intent, they can hardly ignore what passes for intellectual currency in that part of the world where vital decisions are made or what kind of composition succeeds in the terms of that part of the world. Problem formulation and problem

solving, distancing of people, abstraction away from historical circumstance, disappearance of the writer as a being with social attributes, and denial of politics: these are threads that run through
both the textbooks for English 101 and the examples of successful
[liberal foreign policy articles that] I have considered. Perhaps the
similarity goes some way toward explaining the usefulness of our
subject, English, to America. (p. 206)

Besides this connection between freshman English and the
military-industrial complex, we have begun to discover the extensive historical reasons behind whatever ideological stance forms a
subtext in any standard composition class. These influences must
be acknowledged and considered by all of us involved in the
teaching of writing, but they must be considered especially by
those of us involved in setting up or teaching in computer classrooms because of the computer's power to link working writers:
Ignoring that power has serious consequences.

Composition instructors all recognize our profession's more
recent pedagogical alternatives: The more authoritative technique
of focusing an autonomous student writer on a product now exists
alongside one seeking to empower students through process and
collaboration. I hesitate to say that these recent alternatives have
supplanted the traditional practices because of the disagreement I
mentioned earlier in this chapter. Two recent scholars have traced
the origins of the traditional classroom. According to Anne Ruggles Gere (1987) and Karen Burke LeFevre (1987), there are both
historical and political reasons why we traditionally subscribe to
an instructor-centered, noncollaborative classroom and think of
writing as a solitary activity, instead of encouraging process and
collaboration as we teach. The traditional classroom set-up exists
primarily because it mirrors what had been, until recently, the way
we thought we came to know, to receive knowledge. The set-up also
coincides with the traditional view of rhetorical invention (i.e., the
Platonic view of invention) which has prevailed because it is
"compatible with certain assumptions characteristic to Western
capitalistic societies in general and academia in particular"
(LeFevre p. 15).

While Gere discusses theories of knowledge and LeFevre discusses theories of rhetorical invention, they both explain the historical basis for two traditional pedagogical points of view: one

considers knowledge as an entity in itself, something that can be passed along from a "knower" to one less fortunate, and the other views invention as a private property, as opposed to a community construction.

Gere traces the concept of knowledge and points out when significant shifts occurred. In her view, "a fixed and hierarchical concept of knowledge worked against the idea of individuals striving together to create knowledge or to learn. [This] fixed concept derived from the view that knowledge resided in certain sources" (p. 69). Gere finally differentiates between two views of knowledge:

> Knowledge conceived as socially constructed or generated validates the "learning" part of collaborative learning because it assumes that the interactions of collaboration can lead to new knowledge or learning. A fixed and hierarchical view of knowledge, in contrast, assumes that learning can occur only when a designated "knower" imparts wisdom to those less well informed. Implicit in these two views of knowledge are two definitions of language. Seen from the fixed and hierarchical perspective, language is a medium, the vehicle through which knowledge is transmitted. As such it remains on the margins of knowledge. The social constructivist view, by contrast places language at the center of knowledge because it constitutes the means by which ideas can be developed and explored. (pp. 72–73)

So do we believe we learn through language, or do we believe we transmit learning through language? If we believe we are the experts in the class, we subscribe to the hierarchical view of knowledge and would seem to discount that our students, on their own, can communicate effectively with each other in order to learn something—or even to carry it to extreme lengths—can learn something together on their own, which might possibly even surpass what we would have "passed on" to them.

LeFevre explains in part why writing teachers favor and, indeed, clutch at a Platonic view of invention (the idea that truth is accessible by purely individual effort—that inquiry is a private matter). The three major reasons are, according to her, "the influence of literary studies on composition, the persistence of the romantic myth of the inspired writer, and the widespread effects of capitalism and individualism" (p. 15). LeFevre reminds us, first of all, that

Many of us who teach writing come to it by way of a background in literature and literary theory. English departments . . . reinforc[e] the prevailing cultural emphasis on the individual as opposed to the social collective. English professors have tended to be more interested in an individual person or character than a group or social class; more interested in a text than in its relationship to social context; and more interested in the individual, concrete detail than in abstraction and generalization. . . . [M]any of us . . . learned our trade . . . from those who were profoundly influenced by New Criticism. With its claim that an individual text is autonomous and self-contained, New Criticism makes it possible to study a text without knowing facts about the author's life, the author's intention, or the social climate in which the work was composed. The New Critical legacy has accustomed a number of us to looking at individual details or characters, created by an individual author, and occurring in a self-contained text. (pp. 15–16)

Besides explaining where our views of invention come from, LeFevre's theories will prove interesting when examined later in this chapter in connection with hypertext.

The romantic view of the writer, LeFevre's second explanation for the Platonic view of invention,

holds that the writer is inspired from within, as Coleridge claims to have written "Kubla Kahn" in a trance, or as Wordsworth made poems that were a "spontaneous overflow of emotion recollected in tranquility." In the romantic tradition, the inspired writer is apart from others and wants to keep it that way, either to prevent himself and his creations from being corrupted by society, or to maintain a necessary madness . . . that is thought to be, at least in part, the source of art. (p. 17)

Finally, LeFevre addresses the topic of "capitalism, individualism, and invention." "One would expect," she states, "the predominant ideology of a society and its received views about the nature of human thought to affect and reinforce one another." So the work of Soviet psychologists such as Lev Vygotsky and A. R. Luria, swayed by Soviet ideology, "stresses a reciprocal relationship between social activity and individual cognition, accomplished by language." On the other hand, we in America are "influenced by our ideology of capitalism joined with individualism to view invention in both its rhetorical and generic senses as an individual phenomenon" (p. 19).

Collaboration, likewise, has both historical and political reasons for being. A collaborative classroom, in contrast to a hierarchical one, mirrors theories of knowledge espoused principally by a group James Berlin (1982) calls the New Rhetoricians. He calls their ideas Epistemic Rhetoric. Berlin states that the theories of the New Rhetoricians—expressed mainly through the ideas of Ann E. Berthoff, among others—are built on the rhetorics and philosophical statements of people like I. A. Richards, Kenneth Burke, Susan Langer, Ernst Cassirer, and John Dewey (p. 773).

> For the New Rhetoric, knowledge is not simply a static entity available for retrieval. Truth is dynamic and dialectical, the result of a process involving the interaction of opposing elements. It is a relation that is created, not pre-existent and waiting to be discovered. The basic elements of the dialectic are the elements that make up the communication process—writer (speaker), audience, reality, language. Communication is always basic to the epistemology underlying the New Rhetoric because truth is always truth for someone standing in relation to others in a linguistically circumscribed situation. The elements of the communication process thus do not simply provide a convenient way of talking about rhetoric. They form the elements that go into the very shaping of knowledge. (p. 774)

So while some detractors attempt to dismiss collaboration simply as a gimmicky fad, a phenomenon passed down from the 1960s, or to consider it as only one of many neutral pedagogical options open to instructors today, the collaborative classroom in fact presents problems of acceptance because it challenges the assumptions that characterize both capitalistic societies and academia, as well as theories of knowledge reinforced by textbooks built on certain traditions and reactions to those traditions.

Ultimately, choosing to encourage collaboration in a classroom springs from a far, far deeper pedagogical commitment than just introducing an innovative teaching twist. And conversely, choosing to keep a traditional, noncollaborative classroom could mean choosing to run the risk of preventing students from realizing their own power as writers and from challenging the competition, chauvinism, and class structure that have played such a major role in capitalistic societies and academia. A pedagogy presents a way of writing that, as Gere said, embodies a way of knowing the world, a philosophy of the way we think we come to know things.

Such concerns prompted Berlin to argue that the responsibilities of writing teachers far exceed a merely instrumental task of passing along mechanical skill.

> I am . . . concerned . . . that writing teachers become more aware of the full significance of their pedagogical strategies. Not doing so can have disastrous consequences, ranging from momentarily confusing students to sending them away with faulty and even harmful information. The dismay students display about writing is, I am convinced, at least occasionally the result of teachers unconsciously offering contradictory advice about composing—guidance grounded in assumptions that simply do not square with each other. More important, . . . in teaching writing we are tacitly teaching a version of reality and the student's place and mode of operation in it. Yet many teachers (and I suspect most) look upon their vocations as the imparting of a largely mechanical skill, important only because it serves students in getting them through school and in advancing them in their professions. (p. 766)

The choices between the traditional and collaborative pedagogies grow more consequential when we throw a computer classroom into the fray.

Those of us who strive to encourage collaboration in our computer classrooms as well as to seek collaborative software and hardware do so for specific reasons. We understand how crucial both our teaching methods and a computer room's technology are: They bear directly on the ways students come to see themselves as writers and their own writing's power in gaining knowledge. We see and believe that collaboration is not an inconsequential, politically neutral technique.

As far as any steps to or strategies for the gaining of knowledge in a writing classroom, computers seem like no other tool we have encountered until now. Computers *can* change classroom dynamics in our classrooms. But because instructors in a computer classroom have available several pedagogical options with different pedagogical effects, the technology *will not necessarily* change dynamics. We may use the machine for bookkeeping duties such as storing files of assignments and examples students can pick up, as well as use the machine to actually hand out and collect assignments, to capitalize on its word-processing capabilities, and to explain revising strategies more clearly by using an overhead projector connected to the teacher's screen. The pedagogical effect here is that we use the machine to emphasize information and retain authority.

Or we may use the machine as a medium of communication between students: They can pass drafts and messages to each other through a network or file server; they can switch places and add information or introduce complications that the original writer never considered; they can sit in a group around a screen and take turns entering information and developing ideas; they can comment simultaneously as a group on one of the member's papers. The pedagogical effect in this second case is that we remove ourselves from a position of authority in order to challenge the traditional classroom dynamic. We are showing students that they should take some responsibility for their education and needn't feel that one authority knows all the answers. As authors of previous chapters have shown, computers can in this last context demarginalize students traditionally excluded at the boundaries of discourse, validate the contributions of all students, especially those previously silenced because their interaction is impeded by their appearance, gender, class, age, social shyness, or social ineptitude, and allow more creative invention to occur. Computers can allow revision that is as creative as invention, critical, reflective, and unhampered by the secondary concerns of editorial correctness. And they can emphasize the profoundly rhetorical nature of all writing.

After nearly a decade of a conservative national administration unconcerned with enfranchising marginal groups of any sorts, by passing, or indeed, retaining legislation designed to do so, those of us who call ourselves humanists need to question whether we want students sitting in our classrooms to receive the same disenfranchising message from our pedagogies. We need to ask whether students who don't learn from us to value the contributions of the "other" to the making of ourselves, to value networks of communication in expanding our thoughts, will ever learn to value them at all once they leave our university halls where they are supposedly opening themselves to the ideas and ways of the other.

In *A Practical Guide to Computer Uses in the English/Language Arts Classroom* (1987), William Wresch cautions,

> The computer is a capstone for language programs that are already excellent. [But] the computer can also be the death knell for programs that are already in trouble. For teachers who are prone to the workbook view of education, the computer can be a source of endless drill and practice programs on spelling, comma placement, noun identification, and all the rest. Most currently available language arts programs are of this type, so teachers with this bent can quickly collect a bookshelf of electronic worksheets. The computer will be kept busy, and students won't be doing any more writing than they had done before." (p. vi)

Many of us are tempted by this approach when we first face a computer classroom. I was, myself. When asked to help construct a viable curriculum for our computer classroom several years ago, I immediately thought in terms of exercises. I began collecting exercises I wanted to "modify." I scrawled notes to myself asking whether we could get the computer to flag certain words or could figure out a way to get the computer to keep a student from continuing to revise before he made certain changes. I wanted to transfer exercises to disk. I planned to create exercises especially for the computer. But never did I wonder, back then, how I could get students to work together, even though such a collaborative teaching technique plays a major role in both my standard composition and my literature classes; collaboration on the computer never entered my mind.

Without the teacher's intentional guidance, the computer in the classroom can accidentally oppose a pedagogy that in a standard classroom's context empowers students. Transferring a standard composition classroom's syllabus and exercises to a computer classroom will not necessarily involve transferring pedagogy—because the machines change classroom dynamics. For an unaware instructor, class exercises and demonstrations in a computer classroom could form a subtext that betrays a pedagogy of empowerment. Instructors may still dominate the technology in a computer class by allowing the technology to remain teacher-centered. Unaware of pedagogical and ideological issues, then, an instructor might accidentally keep power from the students.

Here at UC Davis we use Appletalk—a file server for the Macintosh. New instructors sometimes erroneously refer to Appletalk as a network and assume that just using Appletalk to hand out or collect assignments means they are using a form of collaboration. But it is not, and they are not. They are simply using the machine to retain authority and to do something that could be done, though not as neatly and with more paper waste, in a standard classroom. Because technology is involved, instructors can feel that their teaching is innovative or new. It *is* new as far as their using machinery in a classroom, but such teaching *is not* new pedagogically. If instructors look critically beyond the technology, they will realize that they are simply being the teacher in the old-fashioned way: they are not encouraging students to interact through the technology. Making this realization, they can then experiment to see whether the software will allow for direct, actual collaboration among students. This particular software does, though not without some experimenting and effort on the instructor's part.

This problem—misperceiving technological use as innovative pedagogy—arose partly because our computer classroom originally had neither a file server nor a network; our problem illustrates the importance of considering a connection between technology and pedagogy when planning a classroom. Because of the technology available for the Macintosh at the time, we never stopped to consider the collaborative aspects of computers. Our problem could also have been partly one that Cynthia Selfe raises: When we were busy trying to set up a new room, a network seemed more like a frill than an integral teaching component. But besides seeming like a frill, a network was technically impossible because no such software had been invented for Macs at the time. Such a problem, however, need not recur unintentionally. In the future, instructors installing computer rooms can ask whether a network exists for the machinery they have chosen. If one does, and if they have any say in designing their classroom, they will know not to install the device last but, instead, right along with the rest of the equipment because of its importance in the classroom's configuration and pedagogy.

Now that our computer classroom actually exists, we have written a manual discussing all the levels of writing we teach in the room. The manual includes exercises collected from many instructors and explains explicitly how to use them in the computer classroom. I don't intend here to minimize the usefulness of such manuals, especially for instructors new to a computer room. But I do want to suggest that we must recognize how such manuals might approach teaching in a computer classroom from a certain pedagogical point of view and thus imply its accompanying ideology: They may exemplify an authoritative approach to teaching. They may also introduce the computer classroom to new instructors in the way that Wresch warned against: simply as a way of doing exercises more conveniently.

The alternatives I have just sketched suggest several important obligations pertaining to instructors' individual situations: when we enter a computer classroom for the first time, we must consciously work to be aware of aspects of our own pedagogies, and we must continue to reflect on their consequences. Once in the classroom, we cannot expect that software itself will automatically accomplish our pedagogical goals; in fact, we should expect that usually it will do the opposite. I am thinking in particular of some software developed recently for the Macintosh. One of the primary features of early versions of this software was its ability to let the teacher "snoop" on students' papers and interrupt when he felt he needed to make a comment. As described in its ads, this program would seem to run exactly counter to what a teacher in a collaborative classroom would want because it over-privileges the teacher and reduces interaction between students to a secondary, minor, or perhaps nonexistent level. At the same time that we examine software for pedagogical biases, we need to pressure companies into making software that demands critical thinking, and we must offer constructive criticism about the pedagogical problems we see with much of the software currently being produced.

We finally also need to realize that most schools can't afford as sophisticated a local area network as ENFI or software like that which the Daedalus company creates (see chapters 1 and 8); quite often networking software won't yet have been created for the systems our schools now have in place. Those doing research need to remember this problem; those of us teaching need to keep in mind our goal of maintaining a discourse community, then to develop our own methods for encouraging interaction and collaboration. (See chapters 4 and 5.) Certainly we need to push whatever systems we have now, experiment with other instructors who know the systems well, and try to discover what our equipment can do, given our pedagogical goals. Even a simple unrestricted file on the file server, where students can freely pass messages and drafts back and forth, is better than nothing at all.

We must remember, then, that in the excitement of setting up computer labs and classrooms, we could become mesmerized by the technology to the point where we forget our pedagogical goals, forget that theory applies in our computer classrooms just as much as if not more than in a standard classroom; and even more crucial, that we fail to consider the politics and social webs surrounding our situations as we use the technology and adapt software. As citizens, adults, and especially humanists, functioning in and for a democracy, we prefer to think of ourselves as citizens who assume responsibility for our actions and the course of our lives within a community. And this is what we must teach our students: to communicate with each other, to cooperate with each other, to solve their problems together in order to improve the quality of their lives. We need to teach students to become accustomed to a group, to grow comfortable with a community of writers, so that they will always feel compelled to seek such a group whenever they write. Most of all, we can encourage two important values in our students: (1) a sense of community which values communication and the views of others and (2) a belief that their own work contributes validly to that dialogue.

"TECHNOLOGY IS AN ARTIFACT OF THE CULTURE."

—Cynthia L. Selfe, comment during the Conference on College Composition and Communication, Seattle, 1989

I think back to the first computers I learned to use. This is what I recall: having to memorize what now seem excruciatingly torturous procedures and byzantine commands for producing a document that would type up and, even more improbable, print out the way I wanted. Then more than now with the ease of microcomputers, some of us felt ourselves abandoned to the mercy of bizarre programs and sadistic programmers who didn't really know what writers needed to produce copy effortlessly. Although microcomputer programming today appears less obviously manipulative, we need to remember that we still use a program and respond to commands *as they have been programmed.* We work with a concept of writing procedures arising from the programmer's view of the writing process and the way in which the particular programmer understands that we improve writing and gain knowledge.

> The programmer acts within a context of language, culture, and previous understanding, both shared and personal. The program is forever limited to working within the world determined by the programmer's explicit articulation of possible objects, properties, and relations among them. It therefore embodies the blindness that goes with this articulation. (Winograd and Flores, 1986, p. 97)

In the context of a composition class, therefore, students look at writing in the way that the individual who designed their word-processing software conceives of the writing process. If MacWrite's programmer, for instance, thinks of writing as a solitary activity, his program will allow the student to "cut" and "paste" and "copy" as she writes and revises. His editing menu, however, will certainly not allow her to request help from her fellow students in the classroom. If the programmer doesn't consider consulting others to be just as valid a part of the writing process as cutting and pasting, his program won't either.

Like their notion of the writing process, students' interactions with their fellow writers are also bound by the programmed technology available for interaction. If their classroom has none, either because our department couldn't afford it or such software had yet to be invented or the administrators felt it was a frill, then students will think of writing as mainly a solitary activity, except when some of them gather around a single screen to comment on a draft—if their instructor happens to have planned such an activity. They may think their writing linked primarily to the teacher in the class if that teacher continually uses a file server only to pass in papers, copy assignments, or see their papers projected from the teacher's terminal. Thus, they leave the classroom thinking of writing as a solitary engagement rather than an activity prompting them to interact with others in order to spark more ideas than they could generate alone. If some of them become programmers, they, in turn, will never automatically build collaborative devices into their word-processing programs because they have not learned from the technology they've been using that collaboration is just as important a writing technique as cutting and pasting.

As a teacher in a writing class, I too am bound by the programmer's view of writing, and I am unlikely to see its shortcomings unless I have clear pedagogical goals or a pedagogy antithetical to this programmer's view of writing. Instead, I will probably accept "the blindness that goes with [his] articulation." Described by some proponents as tools for subverting the traditional classroom emphasis on linear thinking, recently proliferating hypertext packages offer one example. Hypertext, akin to a giant file card storer, not only encourages branched invention, but with information made accessible according to categories generated by the user herself gives a writer great flexibility in invention possibility, then in tracing and recording the pieces of information through which she has navigated. Although I applaud this application, I find myself leery of hypertext.

I feel uncomfortable because hypertext systems appear to privilege information over context, indeed to ignore context. I value the context of writing and consider the connections between pieces of information equally as important as the information itself. Such connections reveal connotations, attitudes toward the relationship created by the connection, and levels of meaning—in fact, reveal the motives behind the language. I feel disturbed because such programs don't ask the user to reflect on the logical relationships between and implications created by certain combinations of information.

Some hypertext packages would allow users to interact with preexisting texts. We could then rewrite novels or solve textual problems as we see fit. I do recognize that these packages would allow us to try out different contexts so we could learn to appreci-

ate the original contexts, connections, and problems. Yet my un-
ease returns. Such software appears to emphasize disposing of the
careful connections authors have built up between pieces of information in order to construct the total context of their argument. It
appears much less to suggest comparing the reconstruction with
the original. Male and female concepts of text may shed some light
here. If the traditional male point of view has seen text as a way of
preserving authority, preserving a canon, preserving ideas so they
may be passed down in a one-way hierarchical relationship, then
hypertext appears to offer a masculine challenge to that idea
because it disrupts notions of linearity, authority, and text-as-
preservation. But if the female point of view sees text as a precisely
constructed context within which ideas are carefully linked, sees
text more as a way for an outsider to find a voice and gain access
to a larger textual dialogue already in progress, then hypertext
appears to violate texts and destroy a writer's participation in the
ongoing dialogue. From such a female point of view, then, authors
(no matter whether male or female) are being silenced, while the
proponents of hypertext tell them they are being collaborated
with by their readers.

Computers clearly arise from a particular social context. What
happens if the very programs and technology we're using arise
from a particularly biased social context? John Markoff (1989)
recently discussed the degree to which males dominate the computer industry—a domination, I assume, including those segments
of the industry concerned with inventing word-processing programs and the hardware associated with those programs.

> Woman and girls use computers; men and boys love them, and that
> difference appears to be a critical reason why computing in America
> remains a predominantly male province.
>
> While legions of women work with computers in their jobs and
> many excel as computer scientists and programmers, they are almost
> without exception bystanders in the passionate romance that men
> conduct with these machines—whether in computer science labora-
> tories, video-game parlors, garages or dens. . . . It is the "hacker,"
> who spurns the real world to master a universe locked inside a
> computer, who has become one of the most vivid male stereotypes of
> the 1980s. . . . "Computers have become the intellectual equivalent of
> sports for boys," said Linda H. Lewis, a professor of education at the

University of Connecticut who studies the impact of one's sex on the use of computers. . . . [One woman], now a computer researcher at the University of California, Irvine who grew up with a love of both computing and mathematics, said she dropped out of graduate school at Massachusetts Institute of Technology because she was unhappy in the male-dominated hackers' environment.

"It was hard to enter that culture as a woman," she said. (pp. A 1-2)

Perhaps our word-processing software is being programmed by those who think not in terms of community but of gamesmanship and competition, of knowledge as passed down through a hierarchy instead of generated through a dialectic.

Men and women conceive of themselves differently in society. In studying male and female relationships, Carol Gilligan (1982) noticed two recurring images men and women used to describe them—one of hierarchy, the other of a web. These images

convey different ways of structuring relationships and are associated with different views of morality and self. But these images create a problem in understanding because each distorts the other's representation. As the top of the hierarchy becomes the edge of the web and as the center of a network of connection becomes the middle of a hierarchical progression, each image marks as dangerous the place which the other defines as safe. Thus the images of hierarchy and web inform different modes of assertion and response: the wish to be alone at the top and the consequent fear that others will get too close; the wish to be at the center of connection and the consequent fear of being too far out on the edge. These disparate fears of being stranded and being caught give rise to different portrayals of achievement and affiliation, leading to different modes of action and different ways of assessing the consequences of choice. (p. 62)

No wonder fewer women "hack." Women don't operate in the isolated, "top gun" hierarchy driving men to one-up their opponents. But the male hackers are the ones creating the programs we attempt to use in our "collaborative" classrooms.

But even aside from this male–female dichotomy, I feel, to recall the words of Karen Burke LeFevre, that I am being returned to the prevailing cultural emphasis of English departments—the emphasis on the individual (here the individual bit of information) rather than the social collective (or the context of an argument) which that information represents. Hypertext asks me to feel more interest in text than its relationship to social context, more interest in individual, concrete detail than its relationship to abstract concepts or analysis. In a New Critical way, a bit of information becomes autonomous and self-contained, capable of linking with any other bit of information, valid in any reconstruction without knowing about my intent, the social climate in which I created my argument, or which that bit of information reflects.

To return to my argument that the programmer's world becomes the world we unknowingly surround ourselves with, I'll examine the visual representation of the Macintosh file server, Appleshare. Innocuously enough named, this program displays a hand spread to hold a tray of a few Macintosh icons for documents and files. The hand clearly belongs to a waiter or waitress meant to serve, as the device is meant to serve, objects or documents from the chef to the diners, or to remove dirty plates from the diners once the meals have been consumed. This pictorial display probably seemed innocuous enough to its creators. Indeed, it is clever when we consider the play on the word *server*. But if we examine the dynamics of the scenario suggested by the server display, we can begin to understand the dynamics implied by the programmer for whatever context in which the file server will be used.

In *Language as Ideology* (1979), Gunther Kress and Robert Hodge explain the covert ideological systems words and pictures reveal. Attitudes of class and gender betray themselves in the ways relationships play out. Thus, attitudes toward objects, relationships between objects, often show an ideological basis, "a projection of social relationships onto a world of objects" (p. 79). The relationship portrayed in the Appleshare picture and the connotations of the word *server* reveal a crucial attitude toward class. First, a human server is a menial, meant to serve, powerless except as a medium between two people. Like a good food server, the file server should also hover nearly invisibly in the background. Just as we usually don't want to carry on extended dialogues with our servers or expect them to participate in the conversation arising at our dinner table, we don't expect the file server to contribute to our thinking or our pedagogy. The programmer of this software clearly felt the link between working writers was nothing more than a service, a function to keep the area clean, transfer minor communications between two people. The display chosen to represent the file server mirrors this programmer's world where communication between writers is not considered collaborative, certainly not charged with the power to generate ideas. This programmer's world, then, becomes ours.

We consequently perceive the technology as being menial, certainly not something to connect one person with another to create knowledge. It's there to make life easier, to eliminate in the case of a composition class paper clutter. Whereas the name of the software is Apple*share*, the connotations of the technology's actual name override the implications of the word *share*. And so, not surprisingly, many times teachers and students often perceive the file server as nothing more than a menial paper shuffler. Without even knowing it, they have accepted into their classroom an object built on an assumption toward writing that may be completely antithetical to theirs.

If we think of a server as carrying a meal from the chef to the diner, the dynamic of that whole transaction gains special significance in connection with the educational theories of Paulo Freire (1985). The chef creates. The diner accepts the creation and consumes it. The chef is the culinary authority. The diners are subservient gastronomic consumers. In the classroom this dynamic translates to the teacher as authority, the students as subservient consumers of his knowledge. The educator transfers knowledge to the students, thereby domesticating them in the way Freire cautions against: Such an instructor sees students merely as vessels he can fill, lost souls he must save (pp. 7–8, 99–108). Many instructors outside a computer classroom would feel this a dangerous dynamic to run their classes on. But whether they want it or not, the technology may very well suggest such a dynamic unless they consciously fight to devise ways to make the file server a tool that encourages interaction and generates ideas.

What I have said above should make clear that we really cannot afford to ignore the politics of the computer classroom because the computer, especially with a proper networking system, can be an extremely powerful tool when it comes to student collaboration and leveling authority. No matter how much we have used collaboration in the past, communication and collaboration on the computer are different, and we need to take advantage of this difference.

On the system, for instance, used by the schools belonging to the ENFI Consortium, students participate in "synchronous group communication." (See chapters 1 and 8 for extended discussions of the situation I sketch below.) A student's paper can appear on the screens of all members of a group, and the students can engage in a critical on-screen dialogue just below the work. Instructors who work with this system have provided positive evidence of the quality of students' written comments over oral ones. The students concentrate more completely on the text they are being asked to evaluate and make substantive editorial suggestions. Even on a system without a true network, students working in groups on a computer are less distracted by those artificial prohibitions I mentioned earlier (appearance, gender, class, age, social shyness, social ineptitude) in considering the quality of a student's work or in commenting on it. And they are not privileging the instructor's comments at the expense of their own.

Kenneth Bruffee (1973), who has written extensively on collaborative instruction, acknowledges that the ability to organize and teach in a collaborative learning situation must be developed over time. "It took me personally," he says, "several years of wrestling with my own compulsion to Teach as I was Taught." Bruffee also stresses that teachers need to

> go about progressively "demythologizing" [themselves] as The Teacher in the traditional sense. Students must see their teacher differently if they are to learn well collaboratively. But it is important to keep in mind that the teacher must see himself differently too. Like students, teachers also carry with them "the influence of failed institutions . . . when [they] set out to create anything new." The teacher will have to be wary of his own tendency (and that of some of his students) to lapse back into the traditional patterns of dominance and passivity. He will find it tempting to "declare [the students] children, rather than adults." This relationship, "which emphasizes and accentuates the [teacher's] strength and the student's weakness . . . the same relationship that exists between an adult and a child," is at the bottom of the human relations which are normal in a traditional class. It is an attitude which is disastrous to collaborative learning." (p. 642)

It is interesting that Bruffee's quotation above contains several phrases from an essay on college admissions procedures by a high school graduate. In this case, the student himself recognizes and fights against being both treated as a child and expected to remain passive while receiving an education. I think the danger of reversion to traditional teaching patterns in a computer classroom looms even greater because students will want to look to the instructor as the authority on the machinery, the one who can teach them all the right technological moves. They will also want to sit comfortably at their single, solitary terminals, writing their own papers. They may occasionally—or even often—ask other students for technical assistance. But such requests are not true collaboration where students think critically together. The mesmerizing capabilities of that little screen need to be fought—intentionally fought by the teacher—or they will simply reinforce the tradition of writer as sole inventor.

"Education for domestication," Freire has said, is an act of transferring "knowledge," whereas education for freedom is an act of knowledge and a process of transforming action that should be exercised on reality (p. 102). The computer classroom's pedagogy, just as that of a standard composition class, ultimately reflects a political stance. By acting as the sole authority in the classroom and by unthinkingly allowing the computer to reinforce this dynamic, the teacher will be training students to accept a culture of silence, of stifled oral communication, a culture based on patterns of dominance and submission, one that also reinforces existing patterns of marginality (Freire 1985, pp. 9, 71–77). The instructor may be teaching invention strategies that ignore the rich resources of collaboration, and composing techniques that fail to account for the technologically interconnected, problematic world in which students must think and function. "In our writing classrooms," Berlin (1982) says, "we continue to offer a view of composing that insists on a version of reality that is sure to place students at a disadvantage in addressing the problems that will confront them in both their professional and private experience" (p. 777). The world we learned to write in is not the world they will be living and writing in.

On the other hand, an instructor aware of the politics of pedagogy can use the computer as a medium for communication and interaction, a tool fostering democratic patterns of exchange, and a tool including those traditionally excluded at the margins of discourse. Neither I nor the instructors I have cited in this chapter are saying that students should never go off and write by themselves or never look to the teacher as one who can help them to learn. We are saying, rather, in Clifford Geertz's (1973) phrase, that "webs of significance"[1] surround the student writer, webs that communication with others can make him aware of. We need to examine the messages our pedagogies convey to our students so that the way we use technology doesn't give a mixed or contradictory message. And, at least in my mind, we need to show them that they can themselves participate in acquiring knowledge. We need to be instructors who reveal for the myth that it is, the tale of the isolated composer as the only "right" way to knowledge. We need to empower our students—who must, after all is said and done, leave our classes to cope with life in the twenty-first century—by using the computer to teach them how much and in what ways "others" always contribute to each "self."

NOTE

1. Geertz uses this term in *The Interpretation of Cultures*: "Believing . . . that man is an animal suspended in webs of significance he himself has spun, I take culture to be those webs, and the analysis of it to be therefore not an experimental science in search of law but an interpretive one in search of meaning" (p. 5).

WORKS CITED

Berlin, James A. "Contemporary Composition: The Major Pedagogical Theories." *College English* 44 (1982): 765–777.

Bruffee, Kenneth A. "Collaborative Learning: Some Practical Models." *College English* 34 (1973): 634–643.

Freire, Paulo. *The Politics of Education: Culture, Power, and Liberation*. Trans. Donaldo Macedo. Massachusetts: Bergin & Garvey, 1985.

Geertz, Clifford. *The Interpretation of Cultures*. New York: Basic Books, 1973.

Gere, Anne Ruggles. *Writing Groups: History, Theory, and Implications*. Published for the Conference on College Composition and Communication. Carbondale: Southern Illinois, 1987.

Gilligan, Carol. *In a Different Voice: Psychological Theory and Women's Development*. Cambridge, MA: Harvard, 1982.

Kress, Gunther, and Robert Hodge. *Language as Ideology*. London: Routledge & Kegan Paul, 1979.

Lanham, Richard A. "Digitizing Some Keywords." Paper given at the Conference on College Composition and Communication, Seattle, March 19, 1989. Copyright 1989 by Richard A. Lanham.

LeFevre, Karen Burke. *Invention as a Social Act*. Published for the Conference on College Composition and Communication. Carbondale: Southern Illinois, 1987.

Markoff, John. "Computers and the Sexes: Women Use the Machines; Men Romance Them." New York Times News Service. Appearing in *The Davis Enterprise* (February 13, 1989): A1–2.

Ohmann, Richard. *English in America: A Radical View of the Profession*. New York: Oxford, 1976.

Winograd, Terry, and Fernando Flores. *Understanding Computers and Cognition: A New Foundation for Design*. Norwood, NJ: Ablex Publishing, 1986.

Wresch, William. *A Practical Guide to Computer Uses in the English/Language Arts Classroom*. Englewood Cliffs, NJ: Prentice-Hall, 1987.

Selected Bibliography

Adler, Mortimer. *The Paideia Proposal.* New York: Macmillan, 1982. (Boiarsky)

Annas, Pamela J. "Style as Politics: A Feminist Approach to the Teaching of Writing." *College English* 47, no. 4 (1985): 360–371. (Flores)

Arms, Valarie, ed. *IEEE Transactions on Professional Communications: Special Issue on Computer Conferencing,* PC-29.1 (March 1986). (Selfe)

Atwell, Nancie. *In the Middle: Writing, Reading, and Learning with Adolescents.* Portsmouth, NH: Boynton/Cook, 1987. (Boiarsky)

Batson, Trent. "The ENFI Project: A Networked Classroom Approach to Writing Instruction." *Academic Computing* (February/March 1988): 32–33 (Selfe; Skubikowski/Elder); 55–56. (Skubikowski/Elder)

———, and M. Diane Langston. "Two Recent Cognitive Studies of ENFI-Based Instruction: Results and Implications." Paper given at the Computers in Writing and Language Instruction Conference, Duluth, MN, August 1–2, 1988. (Langston/Batson)

Becker, Henry Jay. "Using Computers for Instruction." *BYTE* (February 1987): 149–162. (Selfe)

Belenky, Mary Field, et al. *Women's Ways of Knowing: The Development of Self, Voice, and Mind.* New York: Basic Books, 1986. (Flores)

Benveniste, Guy. "New Politics of Higher Education: Hidden and Complex." *Higher Education* 14 (1985): 175–195. (Barker/Kemp)

Berlin, James A. "Contemporary Composition: The Major Pedagogical Theories." *College English* 44 (1982): 765–777. (Handa)

———. "Rhetoric and Ideology in the Writing Class." *College English* 50 (September 1988): 477–494. (Barker/Kemp; Skubikowski/Elder)

Bernhardt, Steve, and Bruce Appleby. "Collaboration in Professional Writing with the Computer." *Computers and Composition* 3, no. 1 (1985): 29–42. (Selfe)

Bowen, Betsy, and Jeffrey Schwartz. "What's Next for Computers: Electronic Networks in the Writing Classroom." Paper given at the annual meeting of the National Council of Teachers of English, San Antonio, November 1986. (Selfe)

Britton, James, et al. *The Development of Writing Abilities (11–18).* Schools Council Research Studies. London: Macmillan, 1975. (Barker/Kemp)

Bruffee, Kenneth A. "Collaborative Learning and the 'Conversation of Mankind.'" *College English* 46 (November 1984): 635–652. (Skubikowski/Elder)

———. "Collaborative Learning: Some Practical Models." *College English* 34 (1973): 634–643. (Handa)

———. "Social Construction, Language, and the Authority of Knowledge: A Bibliographical Essay." *College English* 48 (1986): 773–790. (Barker/Kemp; Langston/Batson)

Bump, Jerome. "Radical Changes in Class Discussion Using Networked Computers." Paper given at the Conference on College Composition and Communication, Seattle, March 15–18, 1989. (Langston/Batson)

Burns, Hugh. "Computers and Composition." *Teaching Composition: 12 Bibliographical Essays*. Ed. Gary Tate. Fort Worth: Texas Christian University, 1987, pp. 378–400. (Flores)

Catano, James V. "Computer-Based Writing: Navigating the Fluid Text." *College Composition and Communication* 36 (1985): 309–316. (Selfe)

Cavalier, Robert. "Video Discs in Ethics and Aesthetics." Paper given at the Computers in Writing and Language Instruction Conference, Duluth, MN, August 1–2, 1988. (Langston/Batson)

Caywood, Cynthia L., and Gillian R. Overing. *Teaching Writing: Pedagogy, Gender, and Equity*. Albany, State University of New York, 1987. (Selfe)

Chen, Milton. "Gender Differences in Computer Use and Attitudes." Paper given at the thirty-fifth Annual Conference of the International Communication Association, Honolulu, 1985. (Selfe)

"Computer Talks to Downs Kids." *Milwaukee Journal* (December 14, 1987): D4. (Selfe)

Cooper, Marilyn. "Theory and Practice: The Case of Technical Communication Programs." Unpublished manuscript. Michigan Technological University, Houghton, 1987. (Selfe)

Cummins, James. "The Role of Primary Language Development in Promoting Educational Success for Language Minority Students." *Schooling and Language Minority Students: A Theoretical Framework*. Los Angeles: Evaluation, Dissemination, and Assessment Center, 1981. (Langston/Batson)

Cyganowski, Carol Klimick. *Magazine Editors and Professional Authors in Nineteenth-Century America: The Genteel Tradition and the American Dream*. New York: Garland, 1988. (Cyganowski)

Daiute, Colette. "Issues in Using Computers to Socialize the Writing Process." *ECTJ: Educational Communication and Technology* 33, no. 1 (1985): 41–50. (Selfe)

Däumer, Elisabeth, and Sandra Runzo. "Transforming the Composition

Classroom." *Teaching Writing: Pedagogy, Gender, and Equity.* Ed. Cynthia L. Caywood and Gillian R. Overing. Albany, State University of New York, 1987, pp. 45–62. (Selfe)

Elbow, Peter. "The Shifting Relationships between Speech and Writing." *College Composition and Communication* 36 (October 1985): 283–303. (Skubikowski/Elder)

Elder, John, Betsy Bowen, Jeffrey Schwartz, and Dixie Goswami. *Word Processing in a Community of Writers.* New York: Garland Publishing, 1989. (Skubikowski/Elder)

Eldred, Janet. "Computers, Composition Pedagogy, and the Social View." *Critical Perspectives on Computers and Composition Instruction.* Ed. Gail Hawisher and Cynthia Selfe. New York: Teachers College, 1989, pp. 201–218. (Selfe)

Faigley, Lester. "Competing Theories of Process: A Critique and a Proposal." *College English* 48 (1986): 527–542. (Langston/Batson)

Fersko-Weiss, Henry. "Electronic Mail: The Emerging Connection." *Personal Computing* (January 1985): 71–79. (Selfe)

Firestone, Shulamith. "On American Feminism." *Woman in Sexist Society: Studies in Power and Powerlessness.* Ed. Vivian Gornick and Barbara K. Moran. New York: Basic Books, 1971, pp. 485–501. (Selfe)

Fishman, Pamela M. "Interaction: The Work Women Do." *Language, Gender and Society.* Ed. B. Thorne, C. Kramarea, and N. Henley. Rowley, MA: Newbury House, 1983, pp. 89–101. (Flores)

Florio-Ruane, Susan. "The Classroom Context." Presentation for "Contexts for Teaching Writing" Conference, April 26, 1987. (Boiarsky)

Foster, David. *A Primer for Writing Teachers: Theories, Theorists, Issues, Problems.* Portsmouth, NH: Boynton/Cook, 1983. (Barker/Kemp)

Freedman, Sarah Warshauer. *Response to Student Writing.* Urbana: National Council of Teachers of English, 1987. (Boiarsky)

Freire, Paulo. *Pedagogy of the Oppressed.* Trans. Myra Bergman Ramos. New York: Seabury Press, 1970. (Flores; Selfe)

———. *The Politics of Education: Culture, Power, and Liberation.* Trans. Donaldo Macedo. South Hadley, Massachusetts: Bergin & Garvey, 1985. (Handa)

Frey, Olivia. "Equity and Peace in the New Writing Class." *Teaching Writing: Pedagogy, Gender, and Equity.* Ed. Cynthia L. Caywood and Gillian R. Overing. Albany: State University of New York, 1987, pp. 93–105. (Selfe)

Fulwiler, Toby. "Writing across the Curriculum." Workshop presented at the NCTE Winter Workshop, Clearwater, FL, January 5–7, 1987. (Langston/Batson)

Gardner, Howard. *Frames of Mind: The Theory of Multiple Intelligences.* New York: Basic Books, 1983. (Langston/Batson)

Geertz, Clifford. *The Interpretation of Cultures.* New York: Basic Books, 1973. (Handa)

George, Diana. "Working with Peer Groups in the Composition Classroom." *College Composition and Communication* 35 (October 1984): 320–326. (Cyganowski)

Gere, Anne Ruggles. *Writing Groups: History, Theory, and Implications.* Published for the Conference on College Composition and Communication. Carbondale: Southern Illinois, 1987. (Barker/Kemp; Handa)

Gilligan, Carol. *In a Different Voice: Psychological Theory and Women's Development.* Cambridge, MA: Harvard, 1982. (Flores; Selfe; Handa)

Giroux, Henry A. *Ideology, Culture, and the Process of Schooling.* Philadelphia: Temple, 1981. (Epigraph)

Gomez, Mary Louise. "Equity, English, and Computers." *Wisconsin English Journal* 29, no. 1 (1986): 18–22. (Selfe)

Gornick, Vivian. "Woman as Outsider." *Woman in Sexist Society: Studies in Power and Powerlessness.* Ed. Vivian Gornick and Barbara K. Moran. New York: Basic Books, 1971, pp. 70–84. (Selfe)

————, and Barbara K. Moran, ed. *Woman in Sexist Society: Studies in Power and Powerlessness.* New York: Basic Books, 1971. (Selfe)

Hairston, Maxine. "The Winds of Change: Thomas Kuhn and the Revolution in the Teaching of Writing." *Rhetoric and Composition: A Sourcebook for Teachers and Writers. College Composition and Communication.* 33 (February 1982): 76–88. (Barker/Kemp)

Hall, Donald, ed. *The Contemporary Essay.* New York: Bedford/St. Martin's, 1984. (Skubikowski/Elder)

Hamill, Pete. "Love and Solitude." *Vanity Fair* 51, no. 3 (March 1988): 125–131, 192. (Schroeder/Boe)

Havelock, Eric A. *Preface to Plato.* Cambridge, MA: Belknap–Harvard, 1963. (Langston/Batson)

Hawisher, Gail. "Studies in Word Processing." *Computers and Composition* 4, no. 1 (1986): 6–31. (Selfe)

Hawkins, Thom. *Group Inquiry Techniques for Teaching Writing.* Urbana, IL: ERIC Clearinghouse on Reading and Communication Skills, National Institute of Education, 1976. (Cyganowski)

Heath, Shirley Brice, and Amanda Branscombe. " 'Intelligent Writing' in an Audience Community: Teacher, Students, and Researcher." *The Acquisition of Written Language: Revision and Response.* Ed. Sarah Warshauer Freedman. Norwood, NJ: Ablex, 1985, pp. 3–32. (Langston/Batson)

Heim, Michael. *Electric Language: A Philosophical Study of Word Processing.* New Haven, CT: Yale, 1987. (Selfe)

Hillocks, George, Jr. *Research on Written Composition: New Directions for Teaching.* Urbana, IL: ERIC Clearinghouse on Reading and Communications Skills and National Conference on Research in English, 1986. (Langston/Batson)

Hiltz, Starr Roxanne. "The 'Virtual Classroom': Using Computer-Mediated Communication for University Teaching." *Journal of Communication* 36, no. 2 (1986): 95–104. (Selfe)

Holmsten, Vicki. "What Is Macy's Anyway? New York Comes to the Indian Reservation via E-Mail." Paper given at the annual meeting of the National Council of Teachers of English, Los Angeles, 1987. (Selfe)

Holvig, Kenneth. "Voices across the Wires through Breadnet and Clarknet." Paper given at the annual meeting of the National Council of Teachers of English, Los Angeles, 1987. (Selfe)

Horner, John R., and James Gorman. *Digging Dinosaurs.* New York: Workman, 1988. (Langston/Batson)

Hoy, David Couzens. "Foucault: Modern or Postmodern?" *After Foucault: Humanistic Knowledge, Postmodern Challenges.* Ed. Jonathan Arac. New Brunswick, NJ: Rutgers, 1988, pp. 12–41. (Barker/Kemp)

Humphreys, David. "A Computer-Training Program for English Teachers: Cuyahoga Community College and the Urban Initiative Action Program." *Computers in English and Language Arts: The Challenge of Teacher Education.* Ed. Cynthia Selfe, Dawn Rodrigues, and William Oates. Urbana, IL: National Council of Teachers of English, 1989, pp. 3–16. (Selfe)

Johnson, David W., et al. "Effects of Cooperative, Competitive and Individualistic Goal Structures on Achievement: A Meta-Analysis." *Psychological Bulletin* 89 (1981): 47–62. (Barker/Kemp)

Kemp, Fred. "The User-Friendly Fallacy." *College Composition and Communication* 38 (February 1987): 32–39. (Skubikowski/Elder)

Kiesler, Sara, Jane Siegel, and Timothy W. McGuire. "Social Psychological Aspects of Computer-Mediated Communication." *American Psychologist* 39 (1984): 1123–1134. (Selfe)

Knoblauch, C. H., and Lil Brannon. *Rhetorical Traditions and the Teaching of Writing.* Portsmouth, NH: Boynton/Cook, 1984. (Langston/Batson)

Kremers, Marshall. "Adams Sherman Hill meets ENFI: An Inquiry and a Retrospective." *Computers and Composition* 5, no. 3 (1988): 69–77. (Langston/Batson)

Kress, Gunther, and Robert Hodge. *Language as Ideology.* London: Routledge & Kegan Paul, 1979. (Handa)

Laffey, James M. "The Assessment of Involvement with School Work among Urban High School Students." *Journal of Educational Psychology* 74 (1982): 62–71. (Langston/Batson)

Lakoff, George, and Mark Johnson. *Metaphors We Live By.* Chicago: University of Chicago, 1980. (Langston/Batson)

Lakoff, Robin. *Language and Woman's Place.* New York: Harper & Row, 1975. (Flores)

Lanham, Richard. "Convergent Pressures: Social, Technological, Theoretical." Paper presented at the Conference on the Future of Doctoral Studies in English, Wayzata, MN, April 1987. (Selfe)

———. "Digitizing Some Keywords." Paper presented at the Conference on College Composition and Communication, Seattle, March 19, 1989. Copyright 1989 by Richard A. Lanham. (Handa)

———. "The Electronic Word: Literary Study and the Digital Revolution." *New Literary History* 20 (1989): 265–290. (Introduction; Schroeder/Boe)

LeFevre, Karen Burke. *Invention as a Social Act.* Published for the Conference on College Composition and Communication. Carbondale: Southern Illinois, 1987. (Barker/Kemp; Langston/Batson; Handa)

Ludtke, Melissa. "Great Human Power or Magic: An Innovative Program Sparks the Writing of America's Children." *Time* (September 14, 1987): 76. (Selfe)

Mabrito, Mark. "Writing Apprehension and Computer-Mediated Writing Groups: A Case Study of the Peer-Evaluation Processes of Four High- and Four Low-Apprehension Writers Face-to-Face versus Electronic Mail." Unpublished dissertation, University of Illinois at Chicago, 1989. (Langston/Batson)

Macrorie, Ken. *Telling Writing.* Rochelle Park, NJ: Hayden, 1970. (Langston/Batson)

Maher, Frances. "Classroom Pedagogy and the New Scholarship on Women." *Gendered Subjects: The Dynamics of Feminist Teaching.* Ed. Margo Culley and Catherine Portuges. Boston: Routledge & Kegan Paul, 1985, pp. 29–48. (Flores)

Malarkey, Tucker. "English the Write Way." *The Washington Post* (May 5, 1987): D5. (Boiarsky)

Markoff, John. "Computers and the Sexes: Women Use the Machines; Men Romance Them." New York Times News Service. Appearing in *The Davis Enterprise* (February 13, 1989): A1–2. (Handa)

Meek, Brock. "The Quiet Revolution: On-Line Education Becomes a Real Alternative." BYTE (February 1987): 183–190. (Selfe)

Meyers, Greg. "Greg Meyers Responds." *College English* 49 (1987): 211–214. (Selfe)

Mielke, Robert. "Revisionist Theory on Moral Development and Its Impact upon Pedagogical and Departmental Practice." *Teaching Writing: Pedagogy, Gender, and Equity.* Ed. Cynthia L. Caywood and Gillian R. Overing. Albany: State University of New York, 1987; pp. 171–178. (Selfe)

Miller, Casey, and Kate Swift. *Words and Women: New Language in New Times.* Garden City, NY: Anchor, 1976. (Selfe)

Mingle, James R. *Challenges of Retrenchment.* San Francisco: Jossey-Bass, 1981. (Barker/Kemp)

Moffett, James. "Writing, Inner Speech, and Meditation." *College English* 44 (March 1982): 231–246. (Skubikowski/Elder)

Moulthrop, Stuart. "In the Zones." *Writing on the Edge* 1, no. 1 (Fall 1989): 18–27. (Schroeder/Boe)

Nelson, Cary. "Against English: Theory and the Limits of the Discipline." *Profession 87* (1987): 46–52. (Selfe)

Nilsen, Alleen Pace, et al. *Sexism and Language.* Urbana, IL: National Council of Teachers of English, 1977. (Selfe)

Norris, Christopher. *Contest of Faculties: Philosophy and Theory after Deconstruction.* London: Methuen, 1985. (Barker/Kemp)

Ohmann, Richard. *English in America: A Radical View of the Profession.* New York: Oxford, 1976. (Handa)

———. "Literacy, Technology, and Monopoly Capital." *College English* 47 (1985): 675–689. (Selfe)

Olsen, Tillie. *Silences.* New York: Dell, 1986. (Selfe)

Ong, Walter J. "Literacy and Orality in Our Times." *The Writing Teacher's Sourcebook.* Ed. Gary Tate and Edward P. J. Corbett. New York: Oxford, 1981, 1988, pp. 37–46. (Barker/Kemp)

———. *Orality and Literacy: The Technologizing of the Word.* London: Methuen, 1982. (Langston/Batson)

Osborne, R. J., and M. C. Wittrock. "Learning Science: A Generative Process." *Science Education* 67 (1983): 489–508. (Langston/Batson)

Papert, Seymour. *Mindstorms: Children, Computers, and Powerful Ideas.* New York: Basic Books, 1980. (Barker/Kemp)

Patraka, Vivian. "Notes on Technique in Feminist Drama: Apple Pie and Signs of Life." *Feminist Re-visions: What Has Been and Might Be.* Ed. Vivian Patraka and Louise Tilly. Ann Arbor: The Women's Studies Program of the University of Michigan, 1983, pp. 43–63. (Selfe)

———, and Louise Tilly. *Feminist Re-visions: What Has Been and Might Be.* Ann Arbor: The Women's Studies Program of the University of Michigan, 1983. (Selfe)

Perry, Donna M. "Making Journal Writing Matter." *Teaching Writing: Pedagogy, Gender, and Equity.* Ed. Cynthia L. Caywood and Gillian R.

Overing. Albany: State University of New York, 1987, pp. 151–156. (Selfe)

Pfaffenberger, Bryan. "Research Networks, Scientific Communication, and the Personal Computer." *IEEE Transaction on Professional Communication: Special Issue on Computer Conferencing*. Ed. Valarie Arms. PC-29.1 (March 1986): 30–33. (Selfe)

Pullinger, D. J. "Chit-Chat to Electronic Journals: Computer Conferencing Supports Scientific Communication." *IEEE Transaction on Professional Communication: Special Issue on Computer Conferencing*. Ed. Valarie Arms. PC-29.1 (March 1986): 23–29. (Selfe)

Quinn, Mary A. "Teaching Digression as a Mode of Discovery: A Student-Centered Approach to the Discussion of Literature." *Teaching Writing: Pedagogy, Gender, and Equity*. Ed. Cynthia L. Caywood and Gillian R. Overing. Albany: State University of New York, 1987, pp. 123–134. (Selfe)

Rabinowitz, Paula. "Naming, Magic, and Documentary: The Subversion of the Narrative in *Song of Solomon, Ceremony*, and *China Men*." *Feminist Re-visions: What Has Been and Might Be*. Ed. Vivian Patraka and Louise Tilly. Ann Arbor: The Women's Studies Program of the University of Michigan, 1983, pp. 26–42. (Selfe)

Rich, Adrienne. *On Lies, Secrets, and Silence: Selected Prose 1966–78*. New York: Norton, 1979. (Selfe)

Reinharz, Shulamit. "Feminist Research Methodology Groups: Origins, Forms, Functions." *Feminist Re-visions: What Has Been and Might Be*. Ed. Vivian Patraka and Louise Tilly. Ann Arbor: The Women's Studies Program of the University of Michigan, 1983, pp. 197–228. (Selfe)

Riesman, D. *On Higher Education: The Academic Enterprise in an Era of Rising Student Consumerism*. San Francisco: Jossey-Bass, 1980. (Barker/Kemp)

Rodrigues, Dawn. "Computers and Basic Writers." *College Composition and Communication* 36 (1985): 336–339. (Selfe)

Rorty, Richard. *Philosophy and the Mirror of Nature*. Princeton, NJ: Princeton, 1979. (Barker/Kemp)

Rose, Frank. *West of Eden: The End of Innocence at Apple Computer*. New York: Viking, 1989. Quoted by Susan Kinsley in *The New York Times Book Review* (May 7, 1989): 14. (Schroeder/Boe)

Sandler, Bernice Resnick. "The Classroom Climate: Still a Chilly One for Women." *Educating Men and Women Together: Coeducation in a Changing World*. Ed. Carol Lasser. Urbana: The University of Illinois, 1987, pp. 113–123. (Flores)

Sargent, Pamela, ed. *Women of Wonder: Science Fiction Stories by Women about Women*. New York: Vintage Books, 1974. (Selfe)

Schriver, Karen A. "Revising Computer Documentation for Comprehension: Ten Exercises in Protocol-Aided Revision." Pittsburgh: Carnegie-Mellon, Communications Design Center, 1984. (Boiarsky)

Selfe, Cynthia L. "Computers in English Departments: The Rhetoric of Technopower." *ADE Bulletin* 90 (1988): 63–67. (Selfe)

———. "Redefining Literacy: The Multi-Layered Grammars of Computers." Paper given at the annual Conference on College Composition and Communication, Atlanta, March 1987. (Selfe)

———, and John Eilola. "The Tie That Binds: Building Group Cohesion through Computer-Based Conferences." *Collegiate Microcomputer* 6, no. 4 (1988): 339–348. (Selfe)

———, and Billie J. Wahlstrom. "Computer-Supported Writing Classes: Lessons for Teachers." *Computers in English and Language Arts: The Challenge of Teacher Education.* Ed. Cynthia Selfe, Dawn Rodrigues, and William Oates. Urbana, IL: National Council of Teachers of English, 1989, 257–268. (Selfe)

———, and Billie J. Wahlstrom. "Computers and Writing: Casting a Broader Net with Theory and Research." *Computers and the Humanities,* 22 (1988): 57–66. (Selfe)

———, and Billie J. Wahlstrom. "An Emerging Rhetoric of Collaboration: Computers and the Composing Process." *Collegiate Microcomputer* 4, no. 4 (1985): 289–295. (Selfe)

Sharan, Shlomo. "Cooperative Learning in Small Groups: Recent Methods and Effects on Achievement, Attitudes, and Ethnic Relations." *Review of Educational Research* 50 (1980): 241–271. (Barker/Kemp)

Shor, Ira. *Critical Teaching and Everyday Life.* Boston: South End Press, 1980. (Barker/Kemp)

Sirc, Geoffrey. "Learning to Write on a LAN." *T.H.E. Journal* 15, no. 8 (April 1988): 99–104. (Langston/Batson)

Smart, William. *Eight Modern Essayists.* New York: St. Martin's Press, 1985. (Skubikowski/Elder)

Sommers, Nancy. Presentation at the Conference on College Composition and Communication, Dallas, 1981. (Boiarsky)

Spender, Dale. *Man Made Language.* London: Routledge & Kegan Paul, 1980. (Selfe)

Spitzer, Michael. "Computer Conferencing: An Emerging Technology." *Critical Perspectives on Computers and Composition Instruction.* Ed. Gail Hawisher and Cynthia Selfe. New York: Teachers College, 1989, pp. 187–200. (Selfe)

———. "Writing Style in Computer Conferences." *IEEE Transaction on Professional Communication: Special Issue on Computer Conferencing.* Ed. Valarie Arms. PC-29.1 (March 1986): 19–22. (Selfe)

Sproull, Lee, and Sara Kiesler. "Reducing Social Context Cues: Electronic Mail in Organizational Communication." *Management Science* 32, no. 11 (1986): 1492–1512. (Langston/Batson)

Steeves, H. Leslie. "Feminist Theories and Media Studies." *Critical Studies in Mass Communication* 4, no. 2 (1987): 95–135. (Selfe)

Stenzel, John, Linda Morris, and Wes Ingram. "The Effects of Minicomputer Text-Editing on Student Writing in Upper Division Cross-Disciplinary Courses: Results of a Study by the Writing Center, University of California, Davis." *Computers and Composition* 6, no. 2 (1989): 61–79. (Schroeder/Boe)

Stine, Linda. "Computers and Commuters: Making a Difficult Connection." Paper given at the annual meeting of the National Council of Teachers of English, Los Angeles, 1986. (Selfe)

Techno/Peasant Survival Manual, The. A Print-Project Book. New York: Bantam Books, 1980. Copyright by Colette Dowling. (Selfe)

Townsend, R. C. "Training Teachers for an Open Classroom." *College English* 31 (1970): 710–724. (Barker/Kemp)

West, Candace, and Don H. Zimmerman. "Small Insults: A Study of Interruptions in Cross-Sex Conversations between Unacquainted Persons." *Language, Gender and Society*. Ed. B. Thorne, C. Kramarae, and N. Henley. Rowley, MA: Newbury House, 1983, pp. 102–117. (Flores)

Winograd, Terry, and Fernando Flores. *Understanding Computers and Cognition: A New Foundation for Design*. Norwood, NJ: Ablex Publishing, 1986. (Handa)

Wittig, Monique. *Les Guérillères*. New York: Avon Books, 1969. (Selfe)

Wresch, William. *A Practical Guide to Computer Uses in the English/Language Arts Classroom*. Englewood Cliffs, NJ: Prentice-Hall, 1987. (Handa)

Zimmerman, Don H., and Candace West. "Sex Roles, Interruptions and Silences in Conversation." *Language and Sex: Difference and Dominance*. Ed. Barrie Thorne and Nancy Henley. Rowley, MA: Newberry House Publishers, 1975, pp. 105–129. (Selfe)

Zinsser, William. *On Writing Well*. New York: Harper & Row, 1985. (Skubikowski/Elder)

Notes on Contributors

THOMAS T. BARKER is Associate Professor of English in the Technical Communications Program at Texas Tech University. He has published work in computers and writing and software documentation in *The Technical Writing Teacher, Computers and Composition, Collegiate Microcomputer,* and the *Journal of Technical Writing and Communication.* He is the editor of a book by Baywood Press, entitled *Perspectives on Software Documentation: Inquiries and Innovations,* and is Word Processing Coordinator for the Texas Project in Writing across the Curriculum. He has been Coordinator of the Microcomputer Classroom in the English Department for the past six years.

TRENT W. BATSON has served on the faculty at Michigan State University, George Washington University, and Gallaudet University in Washington, DC (the national university for deaf students) during his 26 years of teaching and administration in academia. Since 1983 he has focused on computers and writing, and in those years has published numerous related articles in journals and chapters in books as well as making many presentations at conferences. In the general area of computers and writing, his chief work has been in computer networking and, in particular, the social and pedagogical implications of real-time writing on-line. In 1989 he co-chaired the fifth Computers and Writing Conference held in Minneapolis. His ENFI Project, with funding and encouragement from the Annenberg/CPB Project in Washington, DC, has enjoyed national attention and, in 1989, was awarded the EDUCOM/NCRIPTAL award for Best Innovation for underprepared writers. He is currently adapting for deaf children what the ENFI Project has learned working with college writers.

JOHN BOE is currently Acting Director of Composition at the University of California, Davis. He is also a storyteller, a writing teacher, the editor of the new composition journal *Writing on the Edge,* and a writer (having published essays, literary and psychological articles, poems, short stories, and reviews). He is especially interested in Shakespeare, fairy tales, children's literature, and Jungian psychology. He attributes his facility with the computer keyboard to his years of piano playing.

CAROLYN BOIARSKY has combined careers in writing and teaching. She has been a state house correspondent, television newscaster, and freelance writer as well as a high school teacher in Appalachia and the coordinator of the Georgia State University Writing Project. Presently on the English faculty at Illinois State University, she has served as Assistant to the Provost for Academic Computer Planning. She has written for *English Education* and *Activities to Promote Critical Thinking* and has published an open-ended software program, *The Poet's Pen*, to teach elementary students to write diamente, cinquain, and haiku.

CAROL KLIMICK CYGANOWSKI is an Assistant Professor in the English Department and Women's Studies Program at DePaul University, Chicago. She initiated and developed DePaul's computer-assisted writing program, and she chairs the College of Liberal Arts & Sciences Computer Users Committee. Her research interests include computers in collaborative learning and effective relationships between writers and editors. Her book, *Magazine Editors and Professional Authors in Nineteenth Century America: The Genteel Tradition and the American Dream*, was published by Garland in 1988.

JOHN ELDER, a Professor of English at Middlebury College and a faculty member during the summer at the Bread Loaf School of English, specializes in computer networks in writing classes. He has collaborated with Kathleen Skubikowski in designing courses focused on computer networks. Through the Bread Loaf School, Elder has taught courses on teaching writing with computers and has participated in a national network of writing teachers and writing classrooms called BreadNet. He is a co-author of *Word Processing in a Community of Writers*, a textbook for college composition courses, published by Garland in 1989. His primary interests as a teacher and writer are nature writing and the connections between American and Japanese literature.

MARY J. FLORES is an Assistant Professor of English, and Director of Composition, Writing-across-the-Curriculum, and the Learning Center—a peer-tutor staffed Writing Lab and Computer Center—at Lewis-Clark State College in Lewiston, Idaho. Her research and teaching interests include computers and composition, collaborative learning, feminist pedagogy, and nineteenth-century American literature. She is currently completing her dissertation, entitled "Narration and Identity: Melville's First Persons," through the University of Michigan.

CAROLYN HANDA teaches composition and English at the University of California, Davis. In addition to her work on the social and political implications of computers in the writing classroom, she is interested in collaborative learning. Handa serves on the editorial board of *Writing on the Edge*. She also specializes in contemporary American poetry and has published several articles on the work of Elizabeth Bishop. Her research interests include contemporary Irish poetry, especially the work of Seamus Heaney.

FRED O. KEMP is an Assistant Professor of English and the Director of Developmental Writing at Texas Tech University. He has written articles and several commercially published computer programs supporting computer-based writing instruction and theory. As one of the founders of the University of Texas' English Department Computer Research Lab, its associate director for four years, and the founder and president of The Daedalus Group, Inc., an educational software development and consulting company, Kemp has been active nationally in the research and implementation of theory-supported computer-based pedagogies for writing and literature instruction.

M. DIANE LANGSTON is a Senior Technical Writer with ICL North America, an international vendor of office automation systems, in Reston, Virginia. She completed a Ph.D. in Rhetoric at Carnegie-Mellon University in 1989 with a dissertation entitled "Engagement in Writing." She has given papers and published articles and technical reports on engagement, computer-based communication in the writing classroom, computer aids to invention, and online user information.

RICHARD A. LANHAM, Professor of English at UCLA, is the author of *A Handlist of Rhetorical Terms, Revising Prose, Analyzing Prose, The Motives of Eloquence, Literacy and the Survival of Humanism*, and other books. He is currently writing a book on electronic text.

ERIC JAMES SCHROEDER teaches in the English, Integrated Studies, and American Studies departments at the University of California, Davis. He also coordinates the Computers and Composition Program for the English Department. His research interests include popular culture and the literature of the Vietnam War. Although his interest in computers was originally accidental, it now comprises too much of his intellectual and emotional life.

CYNTHIA L. SELFE lives in Houghton, Michigan, where she is an Associate Professor of Composition and Communication in the Humanities Department of Michigan Technological University. Her work focuses on the relationships among writers, writing processes, written text, writing teachers, and computers. Selfe has served as the Chair of the NCTE Assembly on Computers and as a member of the CCCC Executive Committee. She currently serves as the Chair of the NCTE Committee on Instructional Technology, and—along with Gail Hawisher—as an editor of *Computers and Composition: A Journal for Teachers of English.*

KATHLEEN SKUBIKOWSKI is Director of Writing at Middlebury College, where her responsibilities include faculty development, advising the Freshman Writing Program and Freshman Seminar Program, and overseeing the peer-tutor system. She has collaborated with John Elder in setting up computer network-based writing classes. Skubikowski also teaches in the English Department, where one of her special interests is Chaucer, the subject of her Ph.D. dissertation at Indiana University.